LOVING ACROSS THE COLOR LINE

LOVING ACROSS THE COLOR LINE

*A White Adoptive Mother
Learns about Race*

SHARON E. RUSH

ROWMAN & LITTLEFIELD PUBLISHERS, INC.
Lanham • Boulder • New York • Oxford

ROWMAN & LITTLEFIELD PUBLISHERS, INC.

Published in the United States of America
by Rowman & Littlefield Publishers, Inc.
4720 Boston Way, Lanham, Maryland 20706
http://www.rowmanlittlefield.com

12 Hid's Copse Road, Cumnor Hill, Oxford OX2 9JJ, England

British Library Cataloguing in Publication Information Available

Library of Congress Cataloging-in-Publication Data

Rush, Sharon.
    Loving across the color line : a white adoptive mother learns about race /
Sharon E. Rush.
        p.   cm.
    Includes bibliographical references.
    ISBN 0-8476-9912-9 (cloth : alk. paper)
    1. Rush, Sharon.   2. Interracial adoption—United States. 3. Racism—
United States.   4. United States—Race relations.   I. Title: White adoptive
mother learns about race.   II. Title.
HV875.64.R87   2000
305.8′00973—dc21   99-089362

Printed in the United States of America

∞ ™ The paper used in this publication meets the minimum requirements of
American National Standard for Information Sciences—Permanence of Paper
for Printed Library Materials, ANSI/NISO Z39.48-1992.

*For my darling daughter
and all children*

CONTENTS

ACKNOWLEDGMENTS

First and foremost, I want to thank my daughter. I cannot adequately convey what a blessing she is in my life. Someday she will understand how valuable her insights as a child were in helping people understand race. For no one was the lesson more meaningful than it was for me, her loving and devoted mother. My wish for her and for all children is for them to hold onto their spirits and to keep the faith.

I am deeply grateful to my parents for instilling in me the value of racial equality; they are wonderful role models. My sisters' and best friend's constant comfort and encouragement gave me immeasurable strength and confidence.

Without a doubt, two people made this project happen: Joe Feagin and Dean Birkenkamp. Joe's encouragement, insightfulness, and support kept me going during the times I wanted to quit. Joe also introduced the book to Dean, whose suggestions, comments, and enthusiasm were inspirational. I also want to thank Dean for assigning the project to Janice Braunstein, my production editor, and Matthew Bouillion, Dean's assistant; his assistance made everything run smoothly. Patti Waldygo's copyedit provided the final boost to my confidence.

Many friends, colleagues, and students supported me through this project and I am grateful to all of them. Some went beyond reasonable expectations by reading and commenting on many drafts or by spending hours with me talking through specific points. A special thank you to them: Kathy Abrams, Dennis and Peggy Calfee, Nancy Cook, Phyliss Craig-Taylor, Terri Day, Richard Delgado, Nancy Dowd, Alyson Flournoy, Steve Friedland, LaShonda Halloway, Berta Hernandez-Truyol, Gilda Josephson, Suzanne Legare, Lyrissa Lidsky, Liz McCulloch, Ken

Nunn, Chris Slobogin, Norma Spurlock, Max Stearns, Jean Stefancic, John Wagner, Walter Weyrauch, and Danaya Wright.

Dean Richard Matasar provided institutional support for this project, but more important, he always believed in the importance of it. I also thank Jon Mills, my current dean, for his institutional and personal support.

I've exhausted numerous research assistants, each of whom provided excellent skills and warm devotion: Darby Hertz, David Cayce, Traci Dreispel, Patricia Duffy, Juliann Hickey, Shane Rowe, and Derrick Scretchen. In particular, Carter Andersen started this project with me at the end of his first year of law school and stayed with it until his graduation in May 1998.

I thank Mark Bergeron, Mae Clark, Betty Donaldson, Marilyn Henderson, Keith Sanders, Nancy Schmitt, Myrtle Smith, and Carol Velasques for providing the necessary support staff and patience to get the job done.

Finally, the introduction, chapter 7, and the epilogue appeared as an article in *Connecticut Law Review* 32, no. 1 (1999), and is reprinted here with the *Review*'s permission. The courage it took for Brian Baldrate and Julie Fay, the editor in chief and articles editor, respectively, to print the article cannot be overstated, because it is far removed from the traditional law review style.

All of the names used in the book are fictitious and some of the stories have been modified without changing their essence.

LOVING ACROSS THE COLOR LINE

INTRODUCTION

"On your mark. Get set. Go!" yelled the coach, as he let go of the two young girls' shoulders, freeing them to run as fast as they could to the finish line.

"Tie," said the assistant coach as each girl slapped his outstretched hands. Mary and Annie smiled at each other, obviously pleased with their performances and their shared victory. After all, they were teammates and there was no particular glory in defeating your teammate. It was just a fun race.

"Okay, girls. Let's do it again," yelled the coach. "We need to see who's the fastest."

The girls looked at each other, shrugged their shoulders, and—hot, sweaty, and tired from their afternoon of softball practice—reluctantly trudged back down the field. Other parents and I watched as Mary and Annie came zooming down the grass toward the finish line for the second time. The determination on their faces left no doubt that they were both putting everything they had into the race; one of them was going to win this one.

"Tie again," screamed out the assistant coach, smiling in disbelief but with obvious approval. Parents, also happy that the girls had both come up winners again, released their sighs and smiled at each other. The girls tried to catch their breath as they enjoyed another moment of shared victory as teammates.

I called to Mary, my daughter, that it was time to go home, thinking that was the end of practice. But the coach wanted the girls to run yet a third race. I thought it wasn't a good idea—it was getting late, the sun was setting, the girls were tired, and everybody felt good that they had tied twice, evidencing their equal running talent.

"Why can't we leave it at a tie? They're both super runners. Let them enjoy that," I suggested. Other parents shared this sentiment. The coach either didn't hear us or ignored us, because the third race was about to begin. The girls

1

were overly tired and this concerned us as mothers. But the races also had turned an afternoon of fun and camaraderie into one of anxiety and competition. Competing against each other, particularly with such intensity, was new and different and not in keeping with the spirit of the team. As parents, we understood that to continue to push for a winner would unnecessarily hurt the loser. Uncomfortable with the coach's decision, we stared at the starting line where the two girls were set for the third race.

"Go!" shouted the coach.

"Too bad," said the woman standing next me. "Mary got off to a late start." I had noticed it, too, and was not surprised that Mary was a step behind Annie as they crossed the finished line. "Annie wins!" declared the assistant coach. Everyone approached the girls, congratulating them and remarking what great runners they both were. Within seconds of crossing the finish line, though, little eight-year-old Mary turned around, pointed her finger at her coach, and exclaimed, "You held me back. That wasn't fair."

I felt everything slow down, like I was in a movie and the camera had just gone to slow speed. I couldn't believe what I was witnessing: my daughter was too small—literally—to be challenging this huge man. And what was she saying to him? Was I hearing her correctly? In a split second, the dynamics of our softball community were drastically changed.

Mary burst into tears. "Why did you hold me that way?" she kept asking the coach between sobs.

The coach became defensive and suggested Mary was lying. Parents and daughters lingered around, waiting to see what would happen. They turned to me with this look that told me I was supposed to calm down Mary, apologize for her "insulting" behavior, and smooth things over so we could all go home feeling okay about seeing each other at the next game.

But I knew I couldn't say anything to make the situation okay. In fact, my experiences with my daughter have taught me that she probably was not mistaken about being held back. She is often treated unfairly because of her race and she is the only Black person on the softball team. In fact, as soon as Mary made her comment to the coach, I thought, "So that explains it. Here we go again."

"But why would I hold your daughter back?" The coach seemed to get even bigger than he was when my daughter confronted him, as he angrily stomped toward me.

Of course, I didn't know the answer to this question—at least, not as an epistemological matter. On some level, it made no sense that the coach would intentionally give Annie a head start. On the other hand, maybe he was just as tired as the girls, realized this third race wasn't such a good idea after all, and he just wanted a winner and arbitrarily picked one, perhaps without even being aware that he was treating Mary unfairly.

Like everyone else witnessing the incident, perhaps like most people reading this story, I wanted there to be a reason unrelated to Mary's blackness and everyone else's whiteness for my daughter's perception that she had been held back. In my heart, though, I knew she had been treated unfairly because she is Black, but I kept my opinion to myself. I knew I could not say what I was thinking because my proffered explanation would be taken as a serious accusation, which I could not prove and which would only leave everyone feeling even angrier at my daughter—who was already perceived to be a "sore loser."

As other parents collected their belongings, the coach and I continued our increasingly heated argument. He admonished that I needed to teach my daughter how to lose. Before I could respond to this personal attack, my daughter interrupted us, tears continuing to stream down her cheeks: "I know how to lose, Coach. I lose all the time. But the game has to be fair. Let's do it again. I know if you don't hold me, I know I could tie her. I know I could tie her again if it was fair." She was demanding justice and, significantly, she was not concerned with winning.

No more footraces, I thought. This whole thing has gotten out of control. But I was proud of my daughter for standing up to her coach. Clearly, she wasn't a sore loser, she wasn't even interested in winning; she was simply asking to be treated fairly. I looked at the coach and said, "I wish there was something I could say that would help you understand."

"Hey, if you don't like my coaching, then why don't you put her on another team? That would be fine with me. Go ahead. Quit," he invited, getting in the last word before walking away.

My daughter cried for hours after we got home, struggling to understand why her coach would betray her and then get so angry about it when she expressed her feelings.

Many people, especially Whites, may doubt that the footrace incident had anything to do with race, thinking my perception is far-fetched or that I am being overly sensitive, particularly as Mary's mother. Readers, especially Whites, may ask the same question the coach angrily yelled at me: "But *why* would I hold your daughter back?" suggesting by the tone of the question that there is no reason he would do such a terrible thing.

Six or seven years ago, I would have shared this sentiment, even though I was a White liberal who believed in racial equality. My commitment to the Black Civil Rights movement came at a very young age. I share this bit of my background in an attempt to express how deep my feelings are about the "wrongness" of racism and also to illustrate that notwithstanding this, it was not until my daughter came into my life that I truly began to understand how profound and persistent racism is in our society.

As a young girl, I can remember visiting my grandparents in Alabama every summer and being admonished by different relatives never to cross the railroad tracks behind the cornfields because that would have put me in the Black neighborhood, although the warnings were couched in the vernacular of the day. I do not remember whether it was the word itself or the disdain with which it was spoken that disgusted me more. I have no idea why I felt this way, but I wanted to dissociate from people when they started "being ugly," as I called it. I did not even know the word *racism,* let alone have any idea what it meant. But I think the real "moment of awareness" for me came when I witnessed some White children beating up some Black children. As a young girl, watching the Black children being hit overwhelmed me with sadness and I simply knew it was wrong.

Visiting my grandparents brought mixed feelings from that moment on. I could not bear to listen to the ugliness or watch another beating and yet I wanted to cross those tracks. Again, I do not know why. Was it just because I was forbidden to? Did I think I could escape the "ugliness" and beatings, which were painful for me? Did I just want to play with the Black children? Was I the eight-year-old anthropologist who wanted to report back to my relatives that "Y'all've got it all wrong." I do not know why I wanted to cross the tracks, but the feelings about how wrong racism is never went away; they became stronger.

Dr. Martin Luther King's famous march from Selma to Montgomery, Alabama, took place only miles from my grandparents' home when I was thirteen years old. Had I been older and had the resources to get to Montgomery, I would have been right in the thick of that march, which is where I was in 1987 as civil rights advocates marched on Forsyth County, Georgia, to protest its exclusion of Black residents, as I talk about in more detail in chapter 4. Moreover, my commitment to achieving racial equality for Blacks and all people of color motivated me to become a lawyer and a law professor. My professional career centers around issues of racial equality: I teach about it, I write about it, and I give public speeches about it. All of my efforts are designed to persuade Whites to join in the struggle for racial equality.

It bears highlighting that despite my lifelong White-liberalist commitment to racial equality and before my daughter and I became a family, it probably would not have occurred to me that the softball coach held my daughter back because she is Black. In fact, years ago, if I had witnessed a similar incident involving a White child and a Black child who was not my daughter, I might have thought what most of the White adults were thinking about my daughter—that she exaggerated what happened. Years ago, I thought I had a keen grasp of racism and believed my knowledge would enable me to maneuver through racial incidents, successfully advocating for my daughter in the White world. I did not realize that my White liberal views on race and race relations were inadequate to comprehend how profound and pervasive racial inequality is in our society. In addition, my "goodwill"—meaning that I did not think I had a prejudiced attitude—was evidenced by my commitment to racial equality and was also supposed to make me a nonracist ally in the colored world. Looking back, I can see that my White liberalism of my predaughter days enabled me to understand the coach's and the other parents' inability to entertain my daughter's accusations. At one time, I suspect I shared with them a common view: We fashioned ourselves people of goodwill and people of goodwill would *never* lay a White hand of oppression on a Black child.

The years with my daughter, however, reveal that being a White person of goodwill is not good enough in the struggle to achieve racial equality. Sometimes I am powerless to mediate the racial incidents involving my daughter. I think back to the afternoon of softball practice and try to imagine what I could have done differently to make the coach and parents understand the relevance of race to the situation.[1] I imagine myself calling a truce with the coach and asking everyone to kindly take their seats in the bleachers and I would try to explain what race had to do with the situation:

Why would the coach hold my daughter back? Let's start with the concept of unconscious racism. The mistreatment of my daughter by White authority figures comports with the phenomenon of "unconscious racism."[2] The coach's behavior may have been motivated by racism, a belief in the inferiority of Blacks compared to Whites. Naturally, none of us think of ourselves as racist—such an ugly word—and this is why the phenomenon is called "unconscious" racism. You, Coach, may not have realized this is what motivated you. Not that it did. (I don't want to make him even more defensive and therefore less open to hearing the lesson.) But just that it might have been the reason and that's worth thinking about. Now I realize that most of you think this is outrageous and believe I am reading too much into the incident. But my point is that the burden of defusing this incident rested on you, Coach. I realize you think Mary's accusation was unjustified, but it nevertheless called for a reflective response as opposed to a reflexive response of calling her a liar. A reflective response would have acknowledged Mary's feelings of betrayal, not just as an eight-year-old, but also as a Black child and the only Black child in our softball community. It was incumbent on you, Coach, primarily as the adult but also as the White authority figure, to dispel any notions that you were prejudiced against Mary because she is Black. Specifically, it is her trust in you that is at issue. If you had said you were sorry that she felt mistreated (even assuming you did not mistreat her), reassured her that you want to be fair to all the girls, and promised that she and Annie could race again at the next practice if they wanted to, perhaps such a reflective response would have eliminated any misunderstandings, especially any misunderstandings that you treated her unfairly because she is Black. Rather than becoming defensive and angry, reflecting on Mary's comment would have allowed you to see that Mary was hurt, confused, and needed your reassurance that you are a fair coach. Even if you disagreed with her comment, a moment of reflection would have allowed room for the importance of her feelings to be validated. A reflective response was the only way for you to win back Mary's trust, assuming that was important to you. Any questions?

Ignoring obvious reasons this scenario would have been absurd, I realize it has taken years of living in an intimate mother–daughter relationship with a Black child for me to uproot my own White liberalism. The parent–child relationship may be the most profound, intense, inexplicable, unconditional love relationship that any two people can share. A natural part of that relationship, particularly with young children, is a mutual need for the other person to be happy, safe, and secure. Parents are especially concerned that their children *thrive* and are acutely emotionally vulnerable when their children are injured, mistreated, or otherwise unable to thrive. Compounding the problem, children are sensitive to their parents' anxiety and frustration as they try to protect children from harm. In this way, children of color suffer double assaults from racism: externally, racism prevents them from thriving by holding them back in all of life's races; internally, they have to cope with the damage racism does to them and to their parents. As a Black mother recently said to me, "I remember the pain on my mother's face and I'm sure my children see it on mine."[3]

White parents of children of color are uniquely situated to contribute to the study of the relationship between White people of goodwill and racism. I am inspired and encouraged by Professor bell hooks's invitation to join in this discourse on race. She writes:

> Luckily, there are individual non-black people who have divested of their racism in ways that enable them to establish bonds of intimacy based on their ability to love blackness without assuming the role of cultural tourists. We have yet to have a significant body of writing from these individuals that gives expression to how they have shifted attitudes and daily vigilantly resist becoming reinvested in white supremacy.[4]

I am writing to tell about my journey from being a person of goodwill to being a person who understands race and racism on a much deeper level because of my experiences as a White mother raising a Black daughter.

My journey also has enhanced my understanding of the relationship between White privilege and its conjoined ideologies of Black domination and subordination. While most people understand how domination and subordination work to oppress Blacks, it is my experience that most Whites do not understand how privilege works to the advantage of White people. Professor Peggy McIntosh defines White privilege as "an invisible package of unearned assets which [a White person] can count on cashing in each day, but about which [she] was 'meant' to remain oblivious."⁵ Understanding the relationship of all three concepts is important in the struggle for racial equality. Professor Adrienne Davis poignantly describes this relationship:

> Domination, subordination, and privilege are like three heads of a [H]ydra. Attacking the most visible heads, domination and subordination, trying bravely to chop them up into little pieces, will not kill the third head, privilege. Like a mythic multi-headed [H]ydra, which will inevitably grow another head if all heads are not slain, discrimination cannot be ended by focusing only on . . . subordination and domination.⁶

In this book, I combine my personal and professional insights on race because together they provide a more complete picture of the dynamics of racism than does either view alone.

In Part I, I explore the practical day-to-day meanings of race based on my experiences with my daughter. All the stories are true and I tell them from a mother's view. I have learned that coping with racism as a mother of a Black child entails far more than a theoretical understanding of race. For example, I explore the relationship between color and race in chapter 1. Closely related, my daughter's identity as a Black girl and the development of her self-esteem are influenced by the color-blind philosophy, as I discuss in chapter 2, and also by her race and gender, as I explore in chapter 5. Many incidents of racial discrimination occur in school, typically thought of as a safe place where children are treated equally. I explore in chapter 3 how far removed from reality this is for Black children and children of color, generally. Similarly, many White people are afraid of Black people and my daughter has not escaped this phenomenon, as the stories in chapter 4 reveal. These stories also reveal a bit of the fear my daughter is learning about, and what it means to be Black in a predominantly White society that values whiteness over all other racial colors.

All the stories reflect our daily struggle against racism. Perhaps parts of my journey will "ring true" for other White people of goodwill and as they learn about these deeper aspects of racism, they will better appreciate how their own views on race may be inadequate to achieve racial equality—an important value to people of goodwill. In turn, perhaps some of them also may be willing to take steps across the color line and be willing to make it easier for people of color to cross the line into privileged White America. Understanding the need to share space[7] with Blacks and all people of color in equal ways is a significant challenge for most Whites. Even one individual can make a difference. The reassurances I receive from audience members, related in chapter 6, encourage me to stay the course.

Part II complements my practical, motherly views of racism as I assume my educator's role and try to put my deeper understanding of racism into theoretical context and also try to put my theory into practical context. The latter is the most important. In my opinion, race relations in America are at an impasse because White society denies racism is a continuing problem, which causes Black society to question America's commitment to equality. In turn, this tension between White denial and Black skepticism has created a deep rift in relationships between Blacks and Whites that is mostly characterized by anger. The cycle of White denial, Black skepticism, and racial anger is developed in chapter 7.

A key component to dismantling racism is to reach the White people of goodwill who are not immediately affected by or involved in eliminating racial injustice, the "ordinary" goodwilled White people of which there are many. My dear friend and college professor Joe Feagin reminded me that almost 500,000 people died fighting over slavery in the Civil War. Among those 500,000 people were many Whites who had lived "ordinary" lives as farmers. Regardless of whether the soldiers were members of the Confederate Army or the Union Army, they were *all* casualties of a society that promoted the grossest form of racial inequality: slavery. Similarly, although current inequality is not manifested in the form of slavery and we are not dying in an official war to end it, *all* of us nevertheless are casualties of today's racial inequality. Two lessons remain as true today as they were during the Civil War. First, racial inequality hurts all Americans, Blacks and Whites, albeit in different ways. Second, racial equality continues to be a core American value that is worth fighting for, and the battle to achieve it cannot be won without a renewed commitment from all White people of goodwill.

Accordingly, chapter 8 suggests two steps White people of goodwill can take to promote greater racial equality for our children of color, our friends of color, and for all Americans of color. First, I suggest that it is important to talk about race to promote greater learning, awareness, and appreciation of racial differences. Creating space for children to talk and learn about race is vitally important, and I explore possible roles teachers can take to help all children reject the precept of Black inferiority and White superiority.

The second step suggests that Whites develop authentic relationships with Blacks. An authentic relationship as I mean it is one in which the people are imbued with equal dignity and respect; one in which all of a person's characteristics, including race, are valued. To this end, it is important for Whites to develop their empathic skills and begin to personally identify with the pain racism causes Blacks and people of color, thereby renewing their commitment to take proactive steps to end racism. The example of Atticus Finch in *To Kill a Mockingbird* comes to my mind.

I also introduce in chapter 8 the idea of transformative love, an emotion more powerful than empathy, and explore what it means and the role it can play in the struggle to achieve racial equality. This new emotion is one I began to feel through my experiences with my daughter as the harm of racism started to affect me directly and in a deeply personal way, and independent of the harm it caused my daughter. Perhaps other Whites who love across the color line and suffer directly from racism will be able to identify with my concept of transformative love.

Perhaps if more Whites better appreciated the profound damage racism does to themselves and to all members of society, especially children, they might be motivated to participate in and allow for two-way travel across the color line, and ultimately support policies and programs that create shared racial space for Americans of all colors. Elimination of the inequality represented by the color line is the challenge for a society that is becoming increasingly multiracial. Most important, this is the challenge for a society that is committed to racial equality regardless of its racial composition.

In undertaking this difficult task, I offer three important caveats. First, I accept that complete racial equality cannot be achieved in American society as it exists today. Yet I also believe that more racial equality can be achieved if (at least some) Whites repudiate their White privilege and actively support equal citizenship for Blacks. By this, I mean that

Blacks and all people of color have the right to participate in American life with equal dignity enjoyed by Whites. Repudiating White privilege is a necessary precursor to a complete dismantling of White supremacy.[8] Initially, it may seem implausible that some Whites would voluntarily repudiate privilege. As one young Black student pressed me at a conference, "But how realistic is it for anyone to voluntarily walk away from power?" My response, perhaps inadequate and overly optimistic, focused on appealing to an essential aspect of humanity—its goodwill toward others.[9]

Understandably, this suggestion seems full of folly. After all, Dr. Alvin Poussaint suggests in his foreword to W. E. B. Du Bois's book *The Souls of Black Folk,* that Du Bois was naive to suppose that he could reason with Whites and appeal to their goodwill to end Black subordination.[10] Specifically, Dr. Poussaint wrote:

> There is constantly the temptation to indulge himself to some extent in the thought that perhaps the problem has never been presented to the white man in a way that he could truly understand, that perhaps *this* time *he* could find a way, a language, a medium for transmitting the urgency of black America to the white man—for surely the progress of civilization has proven that reason can sometimes prevail, illumine, create; and certainly, the alternatives of continuing anguish, hatred, and ultimate suicidal warfare are unbearable![11]

Certainly, I cannot accomplish what Du Bois and other scholars have been unable to accomplish. Still, one must find purpose in trying to end racial subordination,[12] however modest the results prove to be. At times, the frustration is enough to craze anyone who loves someone of color or who cares deeply about equality. As the mother of a Black child, I must make this effort for my daughter and all children. However foolish this project seems, my hope and faith are abiding.[13] My experiences with my daughter tell me that, at the very least, a more solid foundation for achieving equality can be laid by Whites who are willing to step across the color line in the ways I suggest in this book.

More important, most people of goodwill do not want to become coconspirators with people, White or Black, who have internalized the assumption that White America can never repudiate its racism.[14] Professor bell hooks admonishes Black people, "Like our white allies in struggle we must consistently keep the faith, by always sharing the truth that white people can be anti-racist, that racism is not some immutable character flaw."[15] Goodwill Whites who accept racism as a necessary and inevitable aspect of American democracy may think this absolves them of responsibility for helping to end it.[16] In reality, this perspective strips them of their agency,[17] their power to help end racial subordination, an important value to them that is consistent with their goodwill toward others. A person of goodwill would be inclined to repudiate White privilege because she understands her current privilege largely results from the historical subordination of Blacks. In other words, *simply being* White today entitles her to privileges that reflect a continuation of the historical belief in the precept of White superiority and Black inferiority. Unless modern society breaks away from this precept, it cannot sincerely function as a democracy committed to racial equality. To this end, an appeal to goodwill Whites' commitment to equality should be constantly tapped in the struggle.

As I share some of the lessons I have learned about racism from loving my daughter, my second caveat is equally important. As a person of goodwill, I try hard not to be racist. Recently, however, a Black colleague publicly accused me of being racist. I was mortified by the accusation, which was leveled at me in front of a large crowd attending a conference on race. Although I understand that I am racist because I am part of the institution of White privilege, still, my colleague's image of me as a "blatant" racist was out of keeping with my self-image. The embarrassment and hurt I felt overwhelmed my intellectual sensibilities. Unlike the coach, I did not aggressively defend myself, but my reaction was just as ineffective; emotionally, I shut down and, consequently, did not hear much of what my colleague said thereafter. My silent defensiveness caused me to miss an opportunity to learn from my colleague.

Finding an appropriate tone for this book is difficult because I try to move those of us who identify as goodwill Whites into thinking about ways we can talk and learn about race, and also develop authentic relationships with Blacks without also feeling defensive about being White. Defensive Whites may be inclined to "drop out" of the struggle for racial equality. Simultaneously, as much as my self-righteous self wants to believe I would never act like the coach, I am also reminded by my colleague's comment that I may be more like him than I realize or want to be. Goodwill Whites are on constant alert as we try to overcome our own racism but realize we are vulnerable to accusations, often justifiable, that we sometimes get it wrong. I accept Professors Stephanie Wildman's and Adrienne Davis's advice to worry less about "how to avoid that label [racist] . . . and worry [more] about systemic racism and how to change it."[18] As Professor bell hooks writes, "Understanding how racism works, [white people who shift locations] can see the way in which whiteness acts to terrorize without seeing [oneself] as bad, or all white people as bad, and all black people as good."[19] In speaking of "goodwill Whites" in the third person, I try to create a safe distance among the images many of us have of ourselves, the images others might have of us, and the images we aspire to as we move toward repudiating our White privilege so that more racial equality can exist than currently does throughout society.

My final caveat concerns the fact that this book focuses primarily on Whites' construction of racism against Blacks. Certainly, other racial minorities also suffer discrimination[20] and I share my journey with my daughter and offer it as an invitation for others to join in the discussion and share their experiences of loving across the color line.[21] I focus on "White over Black"[22] race relations because my observations stem from my personal experiences with my daughter, whose color is brown and whose biological mother is White and biological father is African American. Her color is important because race in America largely centers around color. As Professor Dorothy Roberts explores in her book *Killing the Black Body*, the darker one's skin color, the less valuable one is perceived to be in America.[23] My personal experiences with my daughter support this observation. For example, when the agency set the adoption fee for my daughter, it offered to cut the fee in half because she is biracial, appears Black, and is harder to place than White babies.

Thus, learning particularities[24] about different racial, ethnic, and other identities better enable us to form coalitions and develop overarching strategies for ending subordination in the myriad forms it takes— from White supremacy to patriarchy and beyond. In turn, our efforts promote equal citizenship for all people.

Part I

A WHITE MOTHER LEARNS
ABOUT RACE AND RACISM

1

COLOR
The Quandary of Race

ON RAINBOWS, KINGS, AND PURPLE PEOPLE

My daughter started making comments at a very young age that told me she noticed color differences among people. For example, when she was five years old, I was a visiting professor at another school hundreds of miles from home. We had just moved into the neighborhood, and a colleague, a single mother with a son the same age as my daughter, planned to visit on a Saturday afternoon. When I told my daughter they were coming, she immediately asked, "What color are they?" I remember thinking that her question seemed odd. Weren't there other things she wanted to know about them—their names? Whether the son liked to ride bikes? Play basketball? Clearly, this type of information was less important to my daughter than knowing their color. I told her she would have to wait and see, but I knew she would be pleased that they were also Black. Sure enough, my daughter saw them walking up the driveway and jumped up and down, exclaiming, "They're Black!"

The glee I heard in my daughter's voice when she realized there were other Blacks in the community told me she was happy she was not going to be the only Black child in town. The joy in her voice also told me something else: perhaps she was beginning to feel some pride in her Blackness. Although she was only five when this occurred, she has not always been so confident and openly happy about being Black. When she was about three years old, I was reading a bedtime story to her— Sleeping Beauty, a version in which all the characters are Black. She

17

stopped me in the middle of the story and asked, "Mom, if black is so special, then why isn't it in the rainbow?"[25] I was not sure how to respond to her. Were we talking strictly about colors or about race? I considered telling her the rainbow did not reflect colors of people. "How many purple people have you seen?" I'd ask her, and she would wrinkle up her nose and giggle and that would be that. A perfect response to an innocent three-year-old's question. But her question was not innocent because she is Black. The rainbow was her metaphor; she was asking me why Blacks do not seem to be as special as people of other colors, especially Whites. When I pointed out that white is not in the rainbow either, I could see her taking in this information, processing it, and reaching some conclusion about whether the rainbow's colors had anything to do with understanding why some skin colors are more valued than others. I could tell that the absence of white in the rainbow was an unsatisfactory response to her, and she still wondered why black was not so special.

We continued with our story of Sleeping Beauty. She liked the part where the prince kissed Sleeping Beauty and woke her up from a deep, deep sleep. This is also my favorite part because it usually occurs right about the time my daughter is falling into a deep, deep sleep, which allows me to kiss her as she peacefully sleeps, much to my weary delight. On this particular evening, though, I knew that race and colors were still on her mind because we did not get much beyond the kiss and Sleeping Beauty's awakening when she popped up from under her Pooh Bear covers, wide awake, and enthusiastically exclaimed, "I have a good idea. Why don't I go and kiss Marfin Lufer King so he can wake up, too!" She literally was smiling from ear to ear, delighted with her idea.

I was amazed by my daughter's insight and her ability to extrapolate from Sleeping Beauty into her own life. We had just celebrated Martin Luther King's birthday, and she had learned he was a famous Black leader who helped other Blacks before he died. The circumstances surrounding his death were best kept for another day when she was older. She watched the news with me and was mesmerized by the television footage of King giving his famous speeches. He clearly made a positive impression on her even at such a young age. She was so proud of her idea to kiss him and awaken him from his deep sleep that I had to keep her from heading out the door to look for him. It took a while longer to get her to sleep that night as I tried to explain the difference between sleep and death, fairy tales and reality to my daughter, who could ask adult questions and had incredible insights but who nevertheless was only three. Just as my response to her rainbow question left her wondering, so, too, did my superficial explanations of death and reality (and I'm not even sure what the latter is). But my explanations were sufficiently boring that she eventually fell asleep. As I kissed her goodnight, I told myself there is time for her to understand race and Martin Luther King's death. What I worried about, however, was whether I would ever be able to stay just one step ahead of her inquisitive and fascinating mind.

After the Martin Luther King incident with my daughter, I asked my friends who are also mothers and fathers if their children were making similar comments about racial color differences. Did they ask why they are White? Hispanic? Asian? Why my daughter is Black? Did they say anything to indicate that they noticed color differences among people? What I learned from my informal poll was that children of color—Blacks, Hispanics, Asians—begin to talk earlier than White children about color differences among people. At least, this was the case for the children in my predominantly White circle. For a short period in their development, then, my daughter and other children of color expressed their awareness of color differences even though the White children were not expressing any awareness they also had of the differences.

I recall when I first flew on an airplane with my daughter. She was only two months old and we were seated next to a young, nine-year-old White girl who was traveling alone. The young girl was fascinated with the baby. When the baby started fidgeting and crying, I told the young girl that she was hungry. The girl got very excited and asked me if I was going to breast-feed her. I'm sure the young girl momentarily thought she had the best seat on the plane. I explained that I couldn't breast-feed my daughter because she was adopted and asked the young girl if she knew what that meant. She immediately smiled and remarked, "So that explains it!" I thought her next comment would have something to do with the racial differences between my daughter and me, but I was mistaken. The young girl continued, "She has straight hair and yours is curly."

The young girl's response was endearing, in many ways, especially since my hair is curly from being permed and my daughter's hair has since become naturally curly. On the other hand, I was not sure what to make of my general observation, consistent with the young girl's comment, that many White children do not talk about color differences among people. Initially, I wondered if White children possess an innocent color-blindness. But my subsequent research taught me something quite different. Social science studies reveal that, in fact, children of all races as young as three are aware of color in people.[26] Moreover, by that young age, White children begin to express negative comments about children of color. Dishearteningly, even children of color who are only three and four years old internalize some of the negativity surrounding their color. This helped me to understand—at least a little bit—why my daughter's perception and the perception of other children of color about their colorfulness generally was *negative* at such a young age. It is not uncommon for children of color to express their wishes to be White; my daughter would make these comments, as many of the stories in this book reveal. What I wondered is how such negativity came to be associated with her Blackness at such a young age? When a child is three, he or she does not even fully understand the concept of "badness." How could it be that children of color feel "bad" about their color?

I am not surprised that some young White children are oblivious to and even confused about color differences among people and what those differences mean. Generally, many adults do not know where race fits into social ordering. Some White adults still espouse White supremacy theories and other White adults promote the color-blind philosophy, suggesting we all act as if everyone is the same color. Naturally, there are many adults between these polar views. Not to be forgotten, of course, are the many goodwill White adults who believe in racial equality but who unintentionally send negative messages about Blacks. These variances among White adults' views on the meaning of race indicate at least one thing: our children receive mixed messages about the value of color differences among people. More important, the general confusion translates into a negative color-consciousness that results in a devaluation of children of color. A recurring theme in this book is that children of color pick up on the negativity and internalize it, and that White children also understand the message to mean that being White is better than being Black. At a very young age, children incorporate adults' ambivalence and, in some cases, adults' negativity about racial minorities, which ultimately lay the foundation for feelings of racial inferiority by children of color and the concomitant feelings of racial superiority by White children.

Naturally, race means much more than color, but color differences seem to be our current social snag. As a society, we do not seem to know what to do with color. Should we value it? Ignore it? Hate it? The ambivalence is highlighted when someone's race does not fit into a specific, definite category. For example, since the adoption of my daughter, I have been constantly presented with this question: Is she a golden-brown Black or a golden-brown White? I could not decide whether to check "African American" or "Caucasian" on her application form for the university's developmental research laboratory school for students in grades prekindergarten through twelfth grade. I hesitated to identify her as only African American because I was uncomfortable defining her solely by the link to her biological father. After all, her biological mother is White, which makes my daughter genetically as White as she is Black. In this way, she and I have a bond that we do not have when it comes to color. It is enormously comforting to my daughter to know that her biological mother and I are both White and we both love her. This information is important because it eliminates, in her young mind, the possibility that her birth mother did not want her because she is Black. Stated alternatively, because I love my daughter's Blackness as a White mother, my daughter has deduced that her White birth mother also must have loved her Blackness. My love is proof positive to a young, adopted child who needs to feel loved by both moms that race had nothing to do with her being placed for adoption.

Additional factors also weighed on my mind as I tried to identify my daughter's race when she was still a baby. Given what I had learned from my studies as a lawyer and professor, I did not want genetics and biology defining my daughter because the genetic definition of race historically was designed for the purpose of making it easier legally to discriminate against Blacks to preserve the purity of the White race; a person who appeared white in color was nevertheless legally classified as Black if there was any "Black blood" in the person's family. In my daughter's case, being "half-Black" during the days of slavery and Jim Crow segregation would surely count as being "Black," regardless of her color. Accordingly, at one time in our history, the government would have *required* White society to discriminate against her. Thus, even at the genetic juncture where the browns, blacks, and golden skin colors seem to fade into whiteness, historically, the law reminded everyone that racial identity is not solely dependent on the visibility of the colorful colors of people. Rather than inviting a deeper inquiry into the meaning of race, the absence of brown, black, or golden skin color quickly focuses attention on biology to provide an easy legal answer to the complex question "What is race?"

The school application exemplifies the difficulty in defining race and it also illustrates how difficult it is to understand what race means. Was the form asking me whether she was *biologically* or *legally* Caucasian or African American? At the time (and she was only a baby), I thought that a "Biracial" box would have solved my dilemma. Even then, I still was not sure what being "biracial" meant outside of genetics, but this was the definition I wanted to avoid because it oversimplified the question. Simultaneously, I also wanted to fill out the form and get her on the list. Because there was no biracial box, I decided at the time that the most accurate way to answer the question of my daughter's race seemed to be to check off both boxes, which was akin to making my own biracial box. Surely, the school officials would know what I meant and might even realize their form needed to be amended to give people more options for racial identification.

Wrong. As insightful as my decision seemed at the time, the school disagreed with it and returned the form with explicit instructions to check off only one square: she is either "African American" or she is "Caucasian." Her application could not be processed until the form was completed, *correctly*. I called the admissions officer and explained my views on trying to identify my daughter's race, expressing my belief that she is both Black and White but the form did not give me this option. Furthermore, I explained that she would develop her own racial identity as she got older and I did not see the need to categorize her at this point in her life. The admissions officer, however, was unpersuaded and suggested that my daughter had a better chance of being admitted into the program as a Black child because they admit children according to percentages based on their race as reflected in the general population in the county.

Although I support affirmative action, I was somewhat uncomfortable accepting the *hint* to identify her as Black to increase her chances of admission to the program. Her racial identity is important and more enduring than the decision I was facing. More important, I did not want her to be admitted or feel like she had been admitted to the school in an unfair way. If she were going to be admitted to the school solely because of her race, then I wanted to have a meeting with the appropriate personnel to discuss any possible ramifications. I struggled for a few days with how to fill out the silly application form, unhappy with either a biological or legal definition of my daughter's racial identity. It was ambiguous from both perspectives and deeper reflection on the meaning of race provided me with even more issues to consider.

As I write this book and look back over the years since I filled out the form, my understanding of the complexities of race make me realize how limited my views were when my daughter was a baby. I have reflected many years on the meaning of race. One of the most difficult aspects of race focuses on political identity. Sometimes a person's color is interpreted by others as a reflection of the person's ideology. On a particular issue, for example, many people are tempted to think that Black people think a certain way about an issue; that Hispanics see it another way; and that White folks see it yet a third way. In its simplest form, this translates into a general belief that there is such as thing as a Black point of view, a Hispanic point of view, a White point of view, and so forth. On some issues, the attachment of a particular viewpoint to a particular race is so strong that when someone violates the settled expectations and expresses a viewpoint inconsistent with the person's racial identity, we tend to realign them with the correct attachment by changing their racial identity. For example, some people, particularly Black people, refer to Supreme Court Justice Clarence Thomas as White because his political positions more closely reflect an ideology associated with White men.

The notion that an individual's political ideology can define the individual's racial identity is problematic. First, most people appreciate being free to have opinions about social and political issues without being prejudged, especially based on characteristics like race. Moreover, the assumption that a person thinks a particular way because of his or her race often leads to other assumptions about the person that have nothing to do with ideology. Such additional assumptions can have quite damaging effects on the individual and members of the individual's group and, generally, such assumptions attach only to non-Whites. For example, many people think lots of Black men are criminals and lots of Black women are on welfare. Generally, such assumptions do not attach to White men and women.

In this way, individual and group identity are related and important, *especially for racial minorities.* For example, it is but a short leap from assuming all members of a particular group think a certain way to a further assumption that they also all lack or possess a particular ability. Some of the stories in later chapters illustrate how my daughter has suffered from certain generalized assumptions many Whites have about Blacks. Stereotypical labeling of people—usually racial and ethnic minorities—does little to foster healthy relationships based on actual knowledge about, or respect for and appreciation of, individuals as individuals and as members of groups.

Returning to the school application, because racial identity is so interrelated to group identity, defining my daughter's race was important. It determined how school personnel would relate to her and also how the entire public school system would view her with respect to all of their policies on race. Thus, to settle the question of her racial identity, I began to think about how other people perceive her. I cannot recount how many times people have remarked how beautiful her color is and asked about her ancestry. While some people ask if she is African American, most people ask if she is Hispanic, West Indian, Oriental, Hawaiian, or even White with a "really deep tan." Almost without exception, when I tell a White person that she is African American, the person responds, "Oh, but she doesn't look it," or "But you'd never know." Moreover, if the person is a woman, she inevitable grabs my arm as she makes her remarks, a typical behavior among women signifying sympathy (as in, "Oh, I'm so sorry to hear that."). Other adoptive parents have even suggested that if they could have "gotten" a baby that looked like my daughter, then they would have been willing to adopt an African American child, too.

I think these types of responses are offered to comfort me and are supposed to be part of the compliment about her beauty. I am supposed to be reassured that most Whites cannot tell the "real" race of my daughter by looking at her. In all honesty, these comments about my daughter's beauty are deeply offensive because they imply that being African American is something to be ashamed of and that if people knew the truth about my daughter, she would no longer be beautiful and people also would think less of her. Comments such as these clearly indicate that to be African American is to be the least beautiful in the eyes of many Whites.

I am happy and proud my daughter is African American and I would not want her to think of trying to "pass" as someone of a different race. Indeed, my primary responsibility as her mother is to build her self-esteem and to make her confident in herself—all aspects of herself, including her racial identity. People can help build the self-esteem of Black children by offering genuine compliments about their beauty and their accomplishments. Remarks that compare one child to another, whether on the issue of race or any other issue, necessarily undermine the sincerity of the compliment and, concomitantly, undermine the child's confidence.

Although it is difficult to identify her race by appearance, in her own eyes as well as the eyes of everyone around her, my daughter is clearly brown. Her color—her *social* race—then, and not her biological or legal race, seems more important in shaping her identity. This is somewhat understandable because her color is visible to everyone and people respond to her as a child of color. My daughter is not White—she is a child of color. All children of color experience life in America from a much different perspective than White children do. This is especially true for African American children, as evidenced by many people's desire to devalue my daughter's African American ancestry and identify her as belonging to a different (which they mean as "more attractive") race.

Thinking about the meaning of race and the application form that literally reduced my daughter's racial identity to a simple black or white question, I decided to check off "African American." Little did I understand then how "right" my choice was. The answer to the question of race was as simple as Black or White but in a *positive* way. My daughter is Black. For those who are curious, she remained on the waiting list for admission to the school for another three years.

The application form did not allow for the fact that race is complex. Recently, I read an interesting article that explained how the "drop of

Black blood" rule has become an empowering bond among African Americans.[27] Originally designed to promote White superiority and Black inferiority, the rule has functioned to reinforce the common history among African Americans and has unified them in their struggle against slavery, segregation, and subordination. To be African American is to be a part of the Black experience in America—an experience that daily causes Blacks to live the effects of their shared history and also provides daily strength in the persistent struggle to achieve racial equality with Whites. Nine years ago, I did not fully appreciate the "correctness" of my decision to check off "African American" on the application and the recent article reminded me that learning about race is an ongoing challenge.

Written many years after I filled out the form, the article explained aspects of race that I did not understand at the time. My daughter's Blackness and African ancestry bond her to other African Americans in their group struggle for equality. Her shared history with them is not a matter of choice for her. Her ancestors' history, coupled with her color and genetic link to her African American father, make her African American.

Over the years I have realized that many people, especially Whites, ignore the complexities of race. This becomes increasingly apparent to me as I try to explain race to my daughter. Explaining race to a young child is almost impossible because it involves so many factors, including biology, law, culture, history, psychology, politics, and social reality. But these are extremely complex concepts, beyond a young child's comprehension. Children's initial understanding of race centers on color—what they see is what they know. To a certain extent this is true for adults as well, although not always. I want to tell a story that adds a whole different dimension to the meaning of race.

My daughter and I were on vacation recently and as we were finishing dinner, a local artist was set up outside the restaurant to draw caricatures of people for a modest fee. The artist had displayed examples of her work and these caught my daughter's eye. Before I knew it, my daughter was sitting to have her portrait sketched by the artist. The artist was very attentive to detail and carefully colored in the intricate patterns on my daughter's shirt and hat. I was impressed with how much time she was willing to take to reflect what my daughter was wearing. When it came time to "color" my daughter's face, the artist turned to me and asked if I was her mother. When I said yes, with much motherly pride, the artist turned to her chalk box, picked out the pink piece, and colored in my daughter's face.

Momentarily, I didn't know what to do. Couldn't the artist see my daughter is brown? The artist had a sketch of Whoopi Goldberg on display, so I knew she was able to draw Black people accurately. I wanted to pull the artist aside and tell her to please color my daughter brown because she is brown and it's important to affirm this part of her identity. Unfortunately, before I could gather my wits to say something, the picture was rolled up and put into its carrying case. I was left with a new definition of race—White mother is pink, Black daughter is pink. The artist defined race by our mother–daughter relationship—even though we are not biologically related, something the artist didn't know. This was the artist's way of coping with the racial differences; she ignored my daughter's Blackness and actually painted her White simply because I was her mother.

Understandably, when my daughter was very young, talks about race focused on color differences. I preferred to discuss color because color is *somewhat* understandable while race is fairly incomprehensible, especially given the infinite variations of racial identity as a matter of biology alone. For example, one of my daughter's camp counselors was curious about my daughter's background and so I explained it. She quickly blurted out that she, too, has a father who is African American and a White mother. My daughter's eyes nearly popped right out of her head in disbelief and joy. Their shared racial background created an instant bond between them.

One day, my daughter was talking to her grandmother (my mother) on the phone and told her about the camp counselor. I overheard my daughter explain to my mother over the phone, "And Kathy's dad is Black and her mom is White. Can you believe it, Granny? And we're the same color." I had to stop what I was doing because my daughter's perception that she and Kathy are the same color did not comport with reality: Kathy is as white as I am and has blondish hair and hazel eyes. It was not even a close call. How likely is it, I asked myself, that my daughter really meant she and Kathy are the same race? Do six-year-olds know about biology and race? Could she know that? Impossible, I thought, but she did understand something about race and that color had something to do with it. Sadly, my daughter's willingness to adopt Kathy's color—White—and claim it as her color, too, reminds me that the battle is constantly on to instill a positive self-image in her as a Black child.

As my daughter matures and gets older, she is gradually moving our discussions about race beyond color and into some of the more abstract aspects of the meaning of race. But only gradually. One especially humorous story illustrates just how gradual the process of understanding race can be. As my daughter and I were driving around town finishing our Saturday morning errands, she asked from the backseat, "So, Mom. If my biological dad had been White, then I would have been White, too. Right?" I answered, "Yes, chances are you would have been White if both of your biological parents were White." I continued, "But remember Kathy, the camp counselor? She appeared white even though her biological dad was Black. If she were to have a baby, her baby might be the same color you are." I thought we were ready to discuss genetics, but her next question took us in a different direction. "So, Mom. How come you care so much about Black people? Why does racial equality matter so much to you?" I reflected a moment, "It just does. You know that I've always been concerned about racial equality. Even when I was your age, I knew it wasn't right to mistreat Black people. I guess you could say I'm Black in my heart. That's it, I have a Black heart."

Immediately, my daughter's head popped between the two front seats, startling me. She exclaimed emphatically, "You're kidding, right, Mom? I mean, I mean, how could you? You don't even smoke!" Before I knew it, the conversation level had reverted to the "literal" world of a nine-year-old and she was telling me all about her science teacher's poster of a pair of black lungs, damaged from smoking, and on and on she went. I chuckled to myself. So much for abstract thoughts about race.

I suspect my daughter's brownness will enhance her growing understanding of what race means just as my whiteness limits mine. My observations are based more on my growing understanding of racism, which is one of the places where the concepts of color and race intersect. For example, a growing number of Whites think society is or should be color-blind. Simultaneously, people of color are constantly coping with racism. One reason my daughter and other young children of color are so acutely aware of their color is because their color is devalued by most of White society—even by people of goodwill, as I explore in Part II. It bears repeating that a general devaluation of children's colors is interpreted by them as a devaluation of them. Racism persists because people are different colors, which is some evidence of how superficially the issue of race is treated. Acting as a proxy for race, color often obviates the need to discuss history, politics, cultural heritage, economic class, social perception, family, or self-identity in trying to understand what race means. Significantly, when a person's color fails to match the person's proclaimed race, like in Kathy's instance where she identified as Black but appeared White, the inquiry into the meaning of race is exposed as the profound quandary that it is.

Race is much more than color, but color is important to racial identity. In this way, the artist was wrong to color my daughter pink, but she was right to think race is more than color. Logically, then, rejecting a color-blind theory is essential to developing a deeper understanding of race. I have studied the theory of the social construction of race, but it is as a White mother of a Black daughter that I have learned how important and beneficial it would be for everyone to understand the dynamics of the social construction of race and its relationship to color. Pursuing this level of understanding about race might alleviate some of the ambivalence many White adults feel about racial issues. If nothing else, it enables us, as a society, to at least talk about race and begin to think about race in positive, constructive ways.

2

RACIAL PRIDE
Color-Blind or Color-Conscious?

ON BEATLES, BUGS, AND POWER RANGERS

When my daughter was three years old, I drove her and one of her White friends home from nursery school. The radio was playing "I Want to Hold Your Hand," one of my daughter's favorite Beatles tunes. I could see the girls in my rearview mirror, nodding along to the music, when my daughter turned to her friend and said, "This is the Beatles. They are black, you know." I noticed my daughter was grinning with delight at her proclamation as she continued to nod her head to the beat of the music. Naturally, I was surprised she could identify the song, but I was completely taken aback by her description of the Beatles. Curious to know what she could be thinking, I asked her why she thought the Beatles were black. She responded, "Don't you remember, Mama? We just saw them at the zoo."

My daughter was doing what many of us do on occasion when she said the Beatles were black. She was associating herself with something positive and claiming it as part of herself. The Beatles song is a lively, happy love song and clearly my daughter and her friend enjoyed singing along with the radio. My daughter wanted to claim some of the good feelings her friend was having by associating herself with the Beatles. Because she thought the Beatles were beetles and therefore black, she used the racial connection to claim the Beatles as one of her own. What she was saying to her friend was, "See, being Black is special; Black people can do amazing things like sing this wonderful song that is making us

31

smile. I'm Black and therefore, I'm special just like the Beatles." Her friend seemed impressed; at least, that's how I interpreted her giggles.

My daughter's perception about the Beatles made me chuckle as I imagined a bunch of beetles singing on the radio and thought how the song would have to be renamed "I Want to Hold Your Hands." I decided to let my daughter revel in her moment of pride and not correct the misunderstanding; as my daughter got older, she would learn the Beatles are men, not bugs, and she would probably never remember she once thought the Beatles were insects. I turned up the radio and we enjoyed her moment of "Black Toddler Pride" as we drove down the streets of our sleepy southern town to her friend's home.

Like most parents, I want my daughter to be proud of herself and to have strong self-esteem. In trying to build my daughter's self-esteem, I have learned that I and other parents of children of color have at least one extra hurdle to overcome compared to parents of White children: when we drop our children off at school or say good-bye to them each morning, we cannot be sure that their self-esteem will stay intact throughout the day. In the case of my daughter, who is still very young and naive, my concerns are twofold. First, I worry about the subtle lessons she is learning about the opportunities available to people of color in society. Second, I worry that the conflicting messages she gets about the value of her Blackness chip away at her self-esteem.

Focusing on the first concern, my daughter has attended three public schools in her short life, the consequence of being the child of a professor who had opportunities to teach at uniquely different schools. Her first public school experience was in Washington, D.C., and the school was remarkably racially and economically diverse. In fact, the racial diversity centered around the children of color who came from many different countries; there were actually very few White students in the school compared to the other public schools my daughter has attended. In the D.C. school, economic limitations and economic privileges seemed to be distributed fairly evenly across students of different races. Although the school was located in a fairly well-to-do part of Washington, students were bused in from other parts of the city to fill empty places in the classrooms.

Her second public school experience came in upstate New York and, as might be expected, the school had a dearth of children of color in attendance. Of those, most were Asian American; there were very few African Americans. There also seemed to be little economic diversity among the students, a consequence of the school's location in a neighborhood mostly inhabited by professional families affiliated with the university.

Finally, in our hometown in the Deep South, she attended one public school in a middle-class, predominantly White neighborhood. In school, there was a racial mixture of children, but the children seemed to be divided by socioeconomic class. As a general observation, the White children seemed to be more privileged than their Black and Hispanic classmates.

Despite the geographical, racial, and socioeconomic differences among the three schools, they all shared a very important common feature. In all three schools, the following positions were held by Whites: principal, school psychologist, nurse, all the teachers with perhaps ten exceptions, teacher aides, most secretaries, sports coaches, and crossing guards. In contrast, during after-school hours, most of the people responsible for the daily upkeep of the physical facilities were people of color—usually Blacks.

My daughter spends most of her time in school, making it an environment that is instrumental in shaping her understanding of the world. She and other children of color are learning important lessons about life that are not part of the official curriculum. One lesson they learn is that very few people of color hold top-level positions in public school education. The corollary to that lesson is that people of color are the janitors, the ones who clean up after the White teachers and administrators.

Remarkably, this scenario has changed only little since the days of enforced legal separation of Black and White children in public education prior to the famous *Brown v. Board of Education* case in 1954. In those days, while the White schools hired janitorial help to keep their schools clean, the parents of the Black children in the Black schools were *expected* to do their own cleaning. This expectation stemmed only from the parents' race; historically, Blacks moved from slaves to janitors. Over time, the association of Blacks with janitorial jobs and janitorial jobs with Blacks became a common stereotype, as if Blacks could achieve no other level of success and as if Whites were above being janitors. Unfortunately, the stereotype is reinforced in the minds of most public school children.

Moreover, the reality of racial inequality extends beyond the school environment and as children become more and more acquainted with the larger world, they will see the same power structure reflected throughout society. It is certainly true at three of the four universities where I have taught. Ironically, I was appointed to my first law school teaching position by a Black dean. It took another fifteen years before I would have another Black supervisor. Indeed, the number of Black colleagues on my faculty can be counted on one hand. The janitorial staff at my school is predominantly, if not all, Black. Significantly, my public law school environment looks a lot like many public elementary school environments. When my daughter comes to work with me, she learns the same lesson about racial inequality that she learns at her schools.

Extrapolating and applying these lessons to the larger world, I wonder how the visible inequality affects Black children's dreams and ambitions. When I attended law school (not that long ago), the faculty had only one woman and one Black professor on it. Without giving it much thought, I deduced that the woman and the Black man were the token minority representatives on the faculty and that it was inconceivable that more women or racial minorities would be hired. Interestingly, I was not even aware of my deduction until my mentor (ironically, the Black professor) suggested that I consider a teaching career. Only then did my unconscious conclusion that only men could be law professors, *with very few exceptions,* surface to my subconscious mind. I responded to his suggestion by asking if he was kidding. Subconsciously, I still believed that only a select few women could be law professors and wondered why he didn't know that.

The significant point, of course, is that my mentor's suggestion that I consider a career in law teaching did not cause me to consciously recognize my own limited thinking about the role of women in law. Like all girls and young women, particularly "in those days," I had been socialized with certain expectations about my ability. I may have been "radical enough" to go to law school, but I was not "radical enough" to be able to see, let alone reject, the precept of female inferiority and male superiority that had been ingrained in me.

Through my experiences as a woman in the predominantly male field of law, I understand how stifling it is to be taught subtle lessons of one's inferiority. When I tell my daughter she can be a school principal or a schoolteacher, what evidence do I have that would persuade her that I am telling the truth? Is my suggestion a joke to her just as my mentor's suggestion was a joke to me? Should I be surprised when she asks if America has ever had a Black man as president of the United States? But imagine her surprised look, given what she sees around her, when I answer that even *she* can be president. "Yes, even a *Black woman* can be president, sweetheart," I have to reassure her. "It won't be easy, honey, because some people think it is better for a man to do the job. And other people think it is better to have a White president. But maybe you can change that." I find myself tempering my responses with a little bit of reality so as to be truthful, but not with so much truth and reality that she gives up hope.

Like parents of White children, I tell my daughter that if she studies, sets goals, and works hard she can be anything she wants to be. Sometimes I can actually show her pictures of Black astronauts, teachers, scientists, doctors, judges, and so forth. I try to include as many Black professionals in our life as possible. But I do not have a lot of examples to show her. Sometimes there are no examples to show her. We all tell our children they can be president, even though probably no parent truly believes his or her child will actually become president. But the doubts parents of children of color hold are different: we doubt White society would elect a president of color, and, even if it did, we doubt it would become such a routine matter that being president would become something all children, regardless of their race, could aspire to with equal hope.

Other parents of children of color probably share my concern about the messages given to our children by the general absence of people of color at the higher end of the economic ladder. Day after day, parents of children of color build up their children's self-esteem, hoping their children will be the lucky ones who break through the racial barriers and become principals, professors, doctors, lawyers, and chief executive officers. For most children of color, however, the days take their toll on their self-esteem as reality catches up to them.

This raises my second concern about the conflicting messages our children get in school about the importance of racial identity. Currently, many White Americans believe that society is or should become color-blind. Often color-blindness is invoked by genuinely caring people who have good intentions; it is supposed to signify that someone does not discriminate against people of color. I, too, believed this at one time. Strong evidence exists, however, to suggest that many genuinely concerned White adults are color-conscious but in negative ways. For example, Professor Joe Feagin, renowned sociologist and expert on race relations, has conducted several studies to measure the attitude of Whites toward Blacks. In almost all of his studies, the data revealed that *most* White Americans (sometimes as many as 75 percent of the respondents) believe in the truth of at least one negative stereotype about Blacks and many of the respondents believe in the truth of more than one negative stereotype.[28]

Many adult beliefs of today undoubtedly were learned by the children of yesterday. Indeed, from my new vantage point across the color line, I can attest to the ways in which our children continue to be indoctrinated in the precept of White superiority and Black inferiority. In an ideal world, because goodwill Whites believe in racial equality, one would think they would adopt the opposite rule of color-blindness and become expressly positively color-conscious. A positive approach to color necessarily eliminates any references to superiority and inferiority. Positive color-consciousness promotes racial equality and obviates the harm that results from being color-blind. Let me try to explain.

COLOR-BLINDNESS

One of my daughter's primary teachers assured me in our initial meeting that she did not even see that my daughter is Black. This is a classic expression of the color-blind philosophy and it came in response to my attempt to talk about my daughter's Blackness with the teacher and try to assess how she viewed the importance of race. The teacher immediately tried to reassure me that she is not racist by exclaiming that she didn't even see my daughter's Blackness.

The teacher meant well by her comment and probably meant that my daughter's Blackness did not cause her to be prejudiced against my daughter. I also knew, however, that the teacher's unwillingness to positively acknowledge my daughter's race was, itself, a form of racism even though she was not fully aware how negative her comments were. This unawareness explains why "color-blind racism" is characterized as unconscious racism. Recall the theoretical lesson I wanted to give the softball community in which I would have tried to explain unconscious racism to the coach and parents. Let me go into more detail here.

Everyone has a color—even White people. When a White person fails to acknowledge the color of a person of color, the White person theoretically renders the person of color White. It is like bleach. Colored clothes that are bleached come out white, not colorless. The teacher did not want to see the Blackness of my daughter so she theoretically bleached my daughter white and proclaimed that my daughter blended in with the White children and herself. By the teacher rendering all the children White, I was supposed to be comforted because she sincerely believed with all her heart that she transcended racism.

In fact, to be color-blind is to be unable to see color. Some people can't tell red from green; we all remember those eye tests. That some people are unable to see some colors (red/green) is one thing; for some people to pretend they do not see black and white is quite another. To be color-blind in the context of racial differences means, *at best*, that a White person sees Blackness but doesn't devalue it or discriminate on the basis of it. But this presents a paradox, a paradox every White person who adheres to color-blindness must confront: Seeing racial differences is inevitable, but if seeing racial differences does not cause one to discriminate against Blacks, then why pretend there are no Blacks in society? The only reason a White person needs to avoid acknowledging a Black person's Blackness is to avoid negative (discriminatory) behavior by the White person toward the Black person. This is a silly trap for unwary White people of goodwill who adamantly insist that they would never knowingly and intentionally discriminate against Blacks anyway.

Generally, then, our children's teachers are genuinely good-hearted and well-meaning and our children (especially the young ones), with rare exceptions, adore them. Still, a teacher's adherence to color-blindness can promote the precept of Black inferiority and White superiority. I certainly worried that my daughter's teacher's color-blind philosophy would hurt my daughter's chances of having a positive self-image as a young Black girl.

However, I did not want to get off to a bad start with the teacher and possibly make it even harder for my daughter to succeed in school. Unconscious racism is a difficult concept and I did not know exactly how to teach the teacher about it without also offending her and creating an awkward and potentially hostile environment for my daughter and other Black children. This is a constant challenge for Whites, made all the more difficult because we have such varied views and levels of understanding about race and racism. I simply didn't know the teacher well enough at the beginning of the school year to delve into the topic. A too-early-in-the-year discussion about race had the potential to be as fruitless and as disastrous as taking a stand in the softball bleachers would have been. I thought it wiser to wait and see how my daughter fared in her class before I said anything about my concerns.

My decision to get to know the teacher and assess the situation was not easy because it temporarily sacrificed my daughter's best interest. Once again, I found myself on the other side of the color line, and as much as I wanted to reach out to the teacher and ask her to cross over that line, I wasn't quite sure how to do it *successfully.* I am well aware of how long it has taken me to cross over the line, and my circumstances are unusual; I am highly motivated to understand race because I love my daughter. Until I figure out how to communicate persuasively with White adults in my daughter's life, inevitably there will be times when I will have to leave her in the care of Whites who believe in color-blindness and unwittingly undermine her self-esteem. Parents of children of color accept this reality everyday.

Living on both sides of the color line is frustrating. Parents want their children to be in environments that *always* bring out the best in them. As adults, we have a responsibility to try and provide our children with optimal environments even though we know this cannot happen *all the time.* But we should be able to get pretty close to making our schools optimal environments for all children. Loving my daughter has taught me that schools are not even close to being optimal environments for her and other children of color. Since becoming a mother, I also appreciate with much greater awareness what parents of Black children are up against as they try to build their children's self-esteem. With little or no warning, unconscious racism knocks the wind out of your child and then out of you—over and over and over again.

My concerns about the teacher's color-blind philosophy were not unfounded. My daughter's best friend, who is White, won the "Student of the Week" award in this particular classroom. My daughter and I talked about what one has to do to receive this award, thinking it might be something my daughter wanted to achieve. However, my daughter seemed genuinely puzzled by our talk. She was not confused about the requirements for winning the award; she knew she had to listen to the teacher, do all her work, help the teacher and other students, and so forth. Her puzzlement came, rather, because she told me she had been doing all these things and did not understand what more she could do.

Her teacher and I had met several times to discuss her progress and I was always told that my daughter was a delight to have in the classroom. These conferences led me to believe that my daughter was eligible for the award. Still, I realized that selecting students for the award was a sensitive issue and truly believed that eventually the teacher would get around to giving every child the award over the course of the year. It was only coincidental, I told myself, that no children of color in the classroom had won the award months into the school year. I told my daughter to be patient and to keep up the good work. I reassured her that she probably would get the award sometime soon, but she was clearly frustrated.

My daughter and I were running late one day and I mentioned that she should hurry so she would not be tardy and jeopardize her chances at winning the award. She had been on her best behavior for several weeks and I felt confident she would win the award soon. While the possibility of winning the award usually worked as a great motivator (parents will use just about anything to get their children going in the morning), this time it did not. My daughter very casually and quietly remarked, without any fanfare at all, "Oh, Mom. Don't you know? I can't win that award. You have to be White to get that."

I remember that her comment stopped me cold. I was just about to sit down in the car and instead, I leaned over the top of the car and looked at her as she stood on our doorstep. I saw a tiny six-year-old Black girl, with her Beauty and the Beast lunch pail swinging from her hand, staring back at me. Apparently, when I stopped getting into the car, she thought she should stop walking toward it. Momentarily, we stood there looking at each other. It was as if the car represented the imaginary color line; she on one side, me on the other. I thought, "Oh, my god, she's so innocent and so young to feel this way. Whatever made her think that?" I was eventually able to compose myself and asked why she thought that. She just shrugged her shoulders.

A shrug of the shoulders seemed at first like a nonchalant response to such a profound observation by a six-year-old. But her response was anything but nonchalant. After making the comment, she walked toward the car with her head down and without her usual energetic bounce. She was at a loss for words and did not want to talk about it. Clearly, she was hurt and saddened by her understanding that she could never get the award *because she is Black*. Still, I wondered where she got this idea. As I dropped her off at school, I walked her to the classroom to make an appointment with the teacher and I learned that her best friend had won the award again.

Admittedly, her best friend is a gem of a student and a charming young girl. Still, I was as puzzled as my daughter that only White children had won the award and that some White children were getting it twice while no Black children were being similarly acknowledged. Like my daughter, I began to wonder if a child of color could get the award. It was impossible that no Black child was deserving of it.

I needed to talk with the teacher about my daughter's understanding that one had to be White to be "Student of the Week." Time for another hard lesson about race and I needed to act quickly because the situation had inflicted a severe blow to my daughter's self-esteem. I played the meeting out in my mind. I raise my concern. The teacher laughs a laugh consistent with her exclamation that "Children can be so silly sometimes, can't they?" She would then remind me that she did not even see my daughter's Blackness and would tell me not to worry, grabbing my arm (that woman thing), indicating the matter is settled. Shortly after our talk, my daughter would win the award, which would prove my daughter wrong and vindicate the teacher.

That was not what I wanted, though. First, parent–teacher confrontations detract from the meritorious value of children's accomplishments and may make children feel incapable of achieving success without parental intervention. In turn, this might damage a child's confidence (not to mention how embarrassed the child might be) and could create anxiety and insecurity in the child.

My most important concern, however, was to ensure that my daughter knew that winning the award was within her ability. She also needed to know that the teacher did not think that being Black made her unworthy of the honor. She needed to know these things with absolute certainty because this knowledge is instrumental to the development of my daughter's self-esteem. If by some fluke she never won the award, she still needed to know that she was worthy of it.

The teacher and I shared responsibility for instilling this knowledge in my daughter. I needed to be able to count on the teacher to help me build my daughter's self-esteem, not tear it down. White teachers live up to their responsibilities as partners with parents of Black children by being positively color-conscious. If my daughter's teacher had not believed in color-blindness and had been positively color-conscious, it would have been highly unlikely that the award could have been withheld from the Black pupils for such a long period of time that at least one of them deduced that her Blackness was an automatic barrier to winning it. For a teacher to create a classroom atmosphere that teaches children the precept of White superiority and Black inferiority, however subtle, is grossly irresponsible.

Another huge concern parents face in situations that call for "out of the ordinary" parent–teacher conferences is that our parental intervention will backfire on our children if teachers become defensive and alienated from us and from our children. Naturally, genuinely good-intentioned White people are hurt and embarrassed when they are accused of being racist because this is at odds with their self-image and with their motives. I was concerned about how to approach the teacher on the awards issue without creating a possible backlash and jeopardizing my daughter's chances for placement in the gifted program.

I remember saying something to the teacher the morning we learned that my daughter's friend had won the award twice, but I cannot remember exactly what I said. I don't recall that my comments focused on race and I am pretty sure they didn't. Instead, I think I made a general remark about how some children hadn't even won the award once, because I do remember the teacher trying to explain why she gave the award to the girl again. Her proffered justification was that the little girl was feeling depressed about something going on in her life outside of school and the girl's mother and the teacher thought that getting the award would cheer her up. I also remember responding that I hoped the little girl felt better and I went ahead and asked to schedule a meeting with the teacher.

Before our meeting, my daughter received the "Student of the Week" award, probably partly because of my implicit suggestion to the teacher that it was unfair to give the award to the same person twice when there were many other deserving students who had not received it even once. I'll never know why my daughter got it when she did, but I do know that her behavior was never as stellar as it was when she wanted to win it and before she thought she could not win it because of her race. Nevertheless, she was proud of herself for achieving this accomplishment and told me she felt like a queen that whole week. I wondered, however, if my daughter came away from the experience with a sense that she was an exception to a rule that one had to be White to get the award. Indeed, my daughter and I got the message that the children of color were less valued than were the White students. Other children, White and Black, inevitably picked up on it, too. The teacher's color-blind philosophy, although well-intended, actually hurt the children.

NEGATIVE COLOR-CONSCIOUSNESS

The primary teacher is not alone in her belief that color-blindness reflects and fosters positive attitudes about race. Many well-intentioned White adults are not aware that their adherence to color-blindness contributes to the negative color-consciousness that permeates society. For example, when my daughter finished soccer camp the summer before second grade, she was given a certificate of participation and several promotional toys by the sponsors of the camp. By far, the most popular item the children were given was a Power Ranger doll. For those unfamiliar with them, the Power Rangers are six seemingly ordinary teenagers who are able to "morph" (metamorphose) into superhuman beings. Once transformed, they wear space-like costumes and have extraordinary strength and agility. They use their superpowers to help people who become victims of evil forces. Each Ranger is a different color; the four young male Rangers are white, black, red, and blue. The young female Rangers are pink and yellow. The romantic element is provided by the white and pink Rangers, who, my daughter reports, are "in love."

At the soccer camp, my daughter was one of two girls in her group of about ten. The reader can probably guess what color Ranger the two girls received, although it is almost too stereotypical to be true. Surprisingly, however, at least one boy also got a pink Ranger. Another boy got a white Ranger and the other boys received Rangers from the other colors.

One almost had to witness the post-camp ceremony to believe what occurred after the children received their packages of goodies from the camp counselors. The boy who got a pink Ranger immediately gave it to a friend so the friend could give it to his sister. The boy who got the white Ranger gleefully yelled to his mother, "I got the white one." Other fellows tried to get him to trade his white Ranger for whatever color they had, but he would hear nothing of it. Meanwhile, my daughter went to the counselor and asked to exchange her pink Ranger for a white one. He let her exchange it, believe it or not, for a black Ranger.

As I watched the pandemonium on the soccer field, I was reminded of an ad I saw as I was browsing through a toy store several years ago when the Rangers just came onto the market. The display in the store advertised, "Buy Four Rangers and Get the White One Free." I had to read the sign again to make sure the word *white* was really there. Sure enough, it was. After seeing the display, several different thoughts went through my mind. First, it was clear the white Ranger must be the easiest one to sell; presumably, this is why it was being used as a "bonus" to induce buyers to purchase four of the other colored Rangers. Clearly, the manufacturer was promoting the white Ranger as the most valuable and conveying this to children, as evidenced by their overwhelming desire to have the white Ranger. It is also true, according to my daughter, that the white Ranger is seen as the boss of the others because he can do more things than the others. When pressed on this, however, she was unable to tell me what the white Ranger could do that the others could not, although the white Ranger is the only Ranger who has a sword in addition to a gun. Her perception of the white one as the "boss" was just something that "everybody knows." In discussing this with a friend, apparently I must be the only one who does not know this. As he told me, the white Ranger not only has the combined strength of the other Rangers, but he also is the "brains" behind the group and plans all their rescues.

Given that there are only six Rangers, however, the toy store's sale guaranteed that the buyer would get all the colored Rangers except one—the one the buyer consciously avoided buying would be the one left behind. By implication and probably by sales statistics, I knew this was unlikely to be the white Ranger. Moreover, for buyers who could afford to purchase four Rangers, perhaps it would not have been much of a financial strain to go all out and get even the fifth Ranger to complete the set. In this way, for some buyers, perhaps many buyers, making the white Ranger "free" may have induced the buyer to purchase all the Rangers. Yet if the advertisement had said, "Buy four Rangers, get one free," the same goal of the manufacturer would have been accomplished. Thus, it was unnecessary to specify in the advertisement that the white one was free, exalting the color white over all the other colors of Rangers. At least three of the other Rangers were colors that people could be—black, yellow, and red—but the message from the sale was that they are not as valuable as the white Ranger. Arguably, the pink Ranger also reflects skin color, but it was made clear to me after soccer camp that the pink reflected more of a gender issue than a race issue. Pink was devalued, not because some people are pink in skin tone—recall that the caricature artist colored my daughter pink after looking at me and learning I was her mother—but because pink represents female and is therefore less powerful.

Significantly, I learned from a friend that the Power Ranger dolls originated in Japan. On the Japanese market, however, there were only five dolls and the white Ranger did not exist. Toy manufacturers created the white Power Ranger (who used to be green) for the United States and other Western markets. This history of the dolls reflects a need by the producers of the dolls to make them more appealing to children and parents in this country. The producers could have made the dolls more American-like in other ways (designed combinations of red, white, and blue uniforms, for example), but they chose to use a racial color and created the white doll to induce American children into buying it and the other Rangers. Ironically, in a society where the prevailing movement is toward color-blindness, even toy manufacturers realize that color is one way children identify with dolls. It is further evidence that children are not color-blind and that adults do not expect them to be. Moreover, it is not coincidental that the white Ranger would have added appeal to a United States market because white is valued over other colors with respect to race.

While the racism in the advertisement for the Power Ranger dolls (indeed, in the whole Power Ranger scheme) is obvious to me and my Black friends who patiently listen to this story, my experience tells me that most Whites will not agree with us and will think we are seeing racism where it doesn't exist. I understand this response because I am only a few years (steps) ahead of them in their understanding of racism; not long ago, I would not have seen the racism. My Black friends, on the other hand, are bewildered that I've been so slow to get it. I can see their bewilderment from the expressions on their faces; they would never be so insensitive as to say something like, "No kidding! Where have you been all these years?" although I would understand it if they did say something like that. I am getting it—slowly, although my learning curve has gone up exponentially since I became the mother of a little Black girl. The soccer camp incident was merely another reflection of the many ways White society sends children very powerful—even if unconscious—messages about their seeming worth as humans based on their color. The soccer incident also evidences a similar devaluation of girls compared to boys, as I explore in more detail in chapter 5.

FROM COLOR-BLINDNESS TO POSITIVE COLOR-CONSCIOUSNESS

It would be silly to suggest to a child that the Power Ranger dolls are all the same color. In the color-blind world of Power Rangers, what color do we tell our children they all are? If we choose to see all the Power Rangers as one color, unless we pick a "neutral" color, a color none of them is, we will favor one Ranger over the others. But if we pick a color that does not reflect any of them, we are exposing the philosophy of color-blindness for the hoax that it is. Moreover, imagine this conversation between a White child and a White parent, who uses the dolls to illustrate the color-blind philosophy of race relations:

Child: "Look, Dad (or Mom). My Red and Yellow Rangers are going on an adventure."

Parent: "How exciting. But you know, of course, your Rangers really don't have any color."

Child: "Huh?" looking quizzically at her dad, as if he had lost his mind.

Parent: "Yes, I know your dolls look like they are Red and Yellow, but they really aren't. At least, in our society we don't talk about the differences in colors between people. In fact, you must learn not to notice the color differences. You can practice with your dolls."

Child: "Huh?" obviously still confused. Then she brightens up, "Oh, I know what you mean. You mean kind of like pretend? We make-believe everybody is the same color?"

Parent: "Yes, like make-believe. You see, we wouldn't want any Rangers to feel bad because they are one color and not another color that everyone might like better, so we just pretend everybody is the same."

Child: "Okay. This is fun, Dad. Let's see. What color should I make them? I'm going to make them all Black!"

Parent: "No, no, sweetheart," looking at his daughter as if she had lost her mind. "I'm guess I'm not being clear. You see, there are Black people in the world and the whole point of pretending not to see colors is so we don't hurt their feelings. How would your Red Ranger feel if he had to pretend to be Black? Don't you think he would be hurt that the Black Ranger doesn't have to pretend to be Red? And that's what I'm trying to explain. We wouldn't want to favor Black over Red because that wouldn't be fair to your Red Ranger. It's the same with people. Take your friend, Billy. Instead of seeing Billy as a Black person, you should try to see him as a person—just like you and me. His Blackness doesn't matter. This way, he won't feel bad about his color . . ."

The conversation between a Black parent and child, of course, would be dramatically different because a Black parent knows how ridiculous and offensive the White parent in the previous story is acting. A Black parent has no incentive to undermine his or her child's identity and confidence. If anything, parents of color are motivated to buy dolls of color for their children so their children can have toys that reinforce their sense of belonging in this culture as children of color. And the toy industry knows this. In recent years, more and more black and brown dolls are on the market and there is a growing demand for them. Even Barbie, the classic and enduring blonde, blue-eyed beauty doll, has an

African American counterpart, as I recently learned and talk about in chapter 5. In reality, the Power Ranger dolls are attractive *because* they are different colors. The color of the individual Power Ranger doll is instrumental to the doll's identity in the child's world.

Unfortunately, the values placed on the dolls generally reflect the value White society places on a person's color. Because Whites enjoy a privileged status in our society, it is not surprising that the white Power Ranger is elevated in importance over the other colored Rangers. Thus, one problem with the Power Ranger dolls is not that they are different colors, but that children learn to value them according to what color they are and internalize the racial messages about White superiority and Black inferiority.

The color-blind philosophy creates tremendous conflict in a Black child's life. The child's family and community revel in their Blackness. Indeed, Black communities are places where Blacks can seek refuge from racism. Imagine the conflict a Black child feels at being a valuable member of a racial community, who is stripped of his racial identity outside of that community. Creating and contributing to this kind of conflict in a child is cruel. Children who receive mixed messages often do not know what they should believe. My daughter tells me that sometimes she feels invisible or like she is "upside down" in the world. When we talk about her feelings, it is clear that she is struggling with precisely this mixed message about the value of her Blackness. She is confused because goodwill Whites avow that they do not see her Blackness and then neglect and mistreat her because she is Black. A child is likely to resolve this dissonance by deducing, quite logically, that Whites do see her Blackness and hate it. Why else would they lie about it? Inevitably, Whites' disdain for her Blackness makes her feel ashamed to be Black. Before long, she is doubting her self and possibly hating her Black self. "If I were White," she deduces (logically), I wouldn't feel this way." Usually, this thought remains silent and what I hear from my daughter is this: "I wish I were White." This audible expression evidences the harsh lessons she has internalized.

Obviously, a color-blind philosophy teaches children of color to disrespect themselves and other people of color. Asking a child to deny his color is asking him to deny a significant part of his identity. Color-blindness fosters a negative self-image among children of color and teaches them not to like themselves. As any educator or responsible adult knows, there is almost no greater damage that can be done to a child than to strip the child of his self-esteem. Yet the color-blind philosophy does just that; it is blind to the needs of children of color.

Equally important and often overlooked by well-intentioned adults is the effect a color-blind philosophy has on White children. The color-blind philosophy engages White children in the conspiracy of disrespect for people of color. After all, the White child learns from goodwill White adults that color does not matter. Simultaneously, the White child also may feel some dissonance between that theoretical message and the message conveyed by the adults' behavior. My daughter's classmates see how the teacher favors White children over Black children. From the White child's perspective, which message speaks louder?

It is virtually impossible to convince children that the world is color-blind—that the Power Ranger dolls are all the same color—because this defies our children's realities. As a mother of a Black child, I do not want to see our society adopt a color-blind philosophy. It would be easy enough to make the Power Rangers all one color, but that would be boring and not as much fun as having them be different colors. I believe the challenge for White adults as toy manufacturers, advertisers, parents, and other responsible adults is to teach our children not to value white dolls (people) over dolls (people) of different colors. Perhaps we should encourage children to use their imaginations to create a world for the dolls in which they exist as a team, working together to achieve various goals. I like to imagine this conversation between a parent and child:

Child: "Look, Mom. My Red and Yellow Rangers are going on an adventure."
Parent: "How wonderful that they can travel together. The Yellow one is so good at hiking through mountains. And, of course, if the Yellow Ranger gets hurt or anything, the Red Ranger can use his medical skills to help his friend. It's always better to travel with a buddy when you are going off on dangerous expeditions. Do you agree?"
Child: "Yeah. Great! And maybe the Pink Ranger can go along too. She's awfully good at decoding secret messages, you know . . . !"

I like this parent–child imaginative play because it makes a positive statement about differences among people. Engaging in conversations or games with my daughter and her friends that affirm racial differences is one way in which I can help them develop positive attitudes about human differences, including race. Adults can use their interpersonal skills and understanding about human differences to affirm children's natural tendency to view dolls as friends who work together to achieve common goals.

I can imagine a society in which children of color do not face the Hobson's choice between self-denial and self-respect; a world in which White children are not torn between White society's color-blind philosophy and children's natural instincts to "call it like it is." Positive color-consciousness helps parents of children of color instill positive self-images in their children. A child who respects himself or herself is motivated to achieve success in healthy ways that continue to produce self-respectful feelings. I want this for my daughter, just as all parents want it for their children, too.

In summary, positive color-consciousness not only comports with reality, but it also reflects the expressed sentiment of goodwilled people. By being positively color-conscious, concerned Whites can check themselves against their own racist thinking. Rather than adhere to the negative stereotypes they learned about Blacks, a positive color-consciousness allows Whites to acknowledge the racist thinking that supports the stereotypes. Consistent with their self-image as people who support racial equality, a positive acknowledgment of racial differences also compels Whites to consciously reject the negative stereotypes of Blacks. Significantly, as positive color-consciousness settles into Whites' way of thinking about race, not only will the precept of Black inferiority disappear, but so, too, will the precept of White superiority because it will have nothing to play off of.

3

BACK TO SCHOOL
The ABCs of Racial Equality

A fter my stay as a visiting professor at the university in upstate New York, my daughter and I returned home in time for her to begin school in the fall. Aware that public schools in our hometown, like most public schools around the country, track students according to traditional criteria about academic ability, I decided to make an appointment with the guidance counselor to talk about my daughter's classroom placement. According to traditional tracking criteria, my daughter would be placed in one of three classes: the "gifted" class, the "regular" class, or the "special needs" class. The gifted class is comprised of students who show "above average" ability, usually determined by their performance on an IQ test. Children who have physical, mental, or other extraordinary needs are grouped together in the special needs classroom. Not to be forgotten, most children are not classified as either "gifted" or "special needs" students and their needs are thought to be met by "regular" classroom placement. As every parent knows, of course, there is no such thing as an "average" son or daughter; each child is wonderfully unique and a parent never has enough time or opportunities to extol the child's talents and virtues.

Many educators believe the three-tier tracking system is the best way to meet the educational needs of all students, but many parents and other educators disagree. They are concerned that the three-tier tracking system erroneously presumes that all children fall into identifiable groups and lack individual talents, abilities, and interests. Moreover, group identification usually centers around the child's ability to perform on a standard IQ test, which measures only math and verbal skills and ignores many other talents and abilities a child might have. For example, a child might be gifted in music or art, but this kind of intelligence does not get evaluated on standard IQ tests. Moreover, standard IQ tests' cultural biases present especially unfair barriers for most children of color, poor people, and girls. The standard IQ indicia of intelligence largely reflects a child's exposure to White, middle-class values peculiar to American culture.

Many children are not exposed to White, middle-class American culture but nevertheless are judged about their intelligence as if they are. For example, one of my students told me a story about a child's experience on an IQ test. The child and his mother had moved here from England and the son was being tested for placement in the American grading system. On the exam, the child had been asked to circle the pictures of words that started with "v" and "st." Among the pictures were a vest and a store. The young boy did not circle those pictures, however, because he had learned that vests are "waistcoats" and that stores are "shops." The boy's decision not to circle the vest/waistcoat or the store/shop comported with his understanding of the world, an understanding that one could not say was wrong. Yet his omissions lowered his IQ test score.

An immediate response to this example (actually raised by a student) might be something to the effect of "Yes, but the boy was English and he should learn about American culture." Inevitably, the young boy will learn about American culture, but this response misses the crucial point. If the purpose of the IQ test is to place the young boy in a program consistent with his ability to grasp materials and learn, then the test's bias toward American values he had not had a chance to learn does not meet his needs. Very intelligent and accomplished adults also can be ignorant about aspects of life to which they have not been exposed. I am reminded of Randall Robinson's (president of TransAfrica) account of his first day at Harvard Law School, which admitted him on full scholarship. Mr. Robinson relates his visit to the school cafeteria where he purchased what he thought was a large doughnut.[29] As he tried to bite into it, he was curious to know why it was so hard and chewy. Stale doughnuts at Harvard? Hard to believe. He was all the more amazed to see a fellow at the next table cover his doughnut in some white stuff. It was not until sometime later that Mr. Robinson learned that the doughnuts were bagels. Mr. Robinson should not be judged less intelligent because he did not know a bagel the first time he ate one. Bagels simply were not a part of his modest upbringing in an African American community. Learning about bagels and cream cheese would be only one new lesson among many he would learn as he acquired more and more knowledge about different aspects of American life away from his community.

It is easy for me to relate to the English boy's and Mr. Robinson's stories because many times I have been in unfamiliar environments and not known quite how to respond. On more than one occasion, not only have I felt insecure in an unfamiliar environment, but I am sure anyone observing me would have seen my insecurities as well. I'll recount only one example, a funny one that even makes me laugh at myself.

Like Mr. Robinson, I was able to attend an Ivy League college but only because my tuition was paid as a result of my mother's ten years of service to the university as a library clerk. My junior year in college, I became friends and ultimately roommates with a woman whose home was in Puerto Rico since her family fled Cuba in the 1960s. One weekend, her parents were visiting the campus and they invited me to a fancy French restaurant for dinner. I was overwhelmed by the invitation. I virtually had no social life at college, partly because I felt out of place being around other kids who were much wealthier than I. Initially, I graciously declined this invitation as well, because I literally did not have anything remotely suitable to wear to a fancy restaurant. But my roommate understood my dilemma and diplomatically suggested I wear one of her dresses. My naiveté and excitement protected me from any awareness of how ridiculous I must have looked in her dress because she was easily four inches taller than I. Her dress draped over me as if I were a clothes rack, and I had to slither along in her high heels to keep them on my feet. But it didn't matter to her or to her family; they wanted me to be with them and share the good time.

Driving to the restaurant, I was a bit uneasy because I didn't know what to expect. Simultaneously, I was also very excited; this was my first night on the town. It wasn't until we arrived at the restaurant and I noticed the place settings at the table that I began to feel terribly uncomfortable. I didn't have a clue what fork or spoon to use or when or how to use them. I didn't know a bread plate from a macaroni plate. As I studied this puzzle of silverware and plate arrangements, my roommate's father ordered champagne cocktails for everyone. I had very little experience with alcohol and had never had champagne in my life. Not wanting to appear "unsophisticated" (ha!), I joined the toasts and drank up. Appetizers? Entrees? Not only had I never heard of the things on the menu, *I couldn't even read the menu.* I deferred to her father's selections. When the huge shrimp cocktail was placed before me, I was baffled as to how I would eat the shrimp. Imagine with all that silverware, I was given yet another fork for the shrimp—a shrimp fork. I laughed. I watched my roommate's mother tackle her shrimp. I mustered up the confidence to try to get one of the huge shrimps into my mouth without spilling the sauce on my roommate's dress. Almost had it, except a violinist had snuck up behind me and when he started playing, I jumped, and my shrimp flew off the fork and landed at his feet. I gasped and was ready to apologize, but he kept playing and smiling at me. Maybe if he didn't see it, no one else had either. I panned the table to see if there were any witnesses. No one was looking at me. Great. I decided to leave the shrimp on the floor and pick it up later. The merriment continued. Wine with dinner? Absolutely! It was part of their culture. From cocktails through dessert, I ate what they ate, drank what they drank, used whatever utensils they used, and I did what everyone else did (I couldn't follow most of the conversation because it was in Spanish or French). And we laughed the night away!

The lack of knowledge about some things that others take for granted is not unusual and it is certainly not indicative of intelligence. It merely reflects experience. It is much more important, in my opinion, that we use our intelligence to learn new things about life and people that might not ever be tested on an exam. When I took my roommate home to meet my parents, she also learned things about modest southern culture that probably were just as eye-opening to her as my journey through her culture had been for me. Instead of eating fancy French dishes and drinking wine, we ate homemade vegetable soup with cornbread and drank iced tea. Remarkably, my college roommate's and my cross-cultural, interracial, and mixed-economic-class friendship has lasted all these years.

The English boy, Mr. Robinson, my roommate, and I represent different slices of life and yet we all have faced standardized tests that were written with "ordinary, White, middle-class Americans" in mind. When an examiner writes the standardized exam, he clearly does not have the four of us and other people like us in mind. The many things we know about because they are part of our everyday life do not appear on these tests. If they did, the "ordinary, White, middle-class American" would get them wrong, not for lack of intelligence, but for lack of knowledge about different aspects of life that they were never exposed to.

In this way, reliance on standard measures of IQ alone as a measure of a child's intelligence promotes inequality among White, middle-class children and other children who do not experience life as reflected in the questions. Not surprisingly, national statistics reveal that children of color are three to four times more likely than White children to be placed in special education classes because of this type of exam bias. Concomitantly, children of color are unlikely to be placed in gifted classes where the student population is overwhelmingly White, again, largely because of exam bias.[30]

Because of this inherent cultural bias favoring White children on the IQ test, my concern about the tracking system only grew as it came time for my daughter to begin school. I wanted to beat the odds that she would be tracked at an inappropriate level because of her race. Unfortunately, this meant working within the three-tier tracking system and trying to ensure she was placed at an appropriate level based on her skills, talents, interests, and abilities as an individual child. Stated alternatively, I needed to ensure that she was not placed in an inappropriate program based on someone else's stereotype of her as a member of a particular group (girls, Blacks, minorities, Black girls). I needed to be actively involved in the placement decision, and hence, my desire to meet with the counselor.

My meeting with the guidance counselor was scheduled for mid-morning. I remember walking up the path to the old-fashioned, red brick schoolhouse, which consumed a whole block in the quiet, tree-lined residential neighborhood. Immediately upon entering the building, I was reminded of my own school days; the floors had that same shine to them as you looked down the long corridors with the two-tone painted walls. Chairs were turned upside down on the students' desks, a sure sign that school was not in session. Off in one corner were construction workers who were trying to fix something up before school started in the fall. The restrooms had signs indicating "Boys" and "Girls," and not the usual "Men" and "Women" signs I was accustomed to seeing in my adult world.

I entered the principal's suite where the guidance counselor's office was located and was introduced to her: a very bright, dynamic, young Black woman. Immediately on meeting her, I was relieved, because I believed she, as a Black woman, would understand what I wanted for my daughter and would be able and willing to help me do what was best for her. Once she learned my daughter's race, surely she would understand that my goal of our meeting was to ensure that my daughter not be tracked in the special needs class where many children of color seem to be placed. As a Black guidance counselor, I just knew that she couldn't, wouldn't let my daughter be misplaced in the tracking system.

As I sat down in the chair across from her in her small, modestly furnished office, I told her the relevant data about my daughter and ended by saying that my daughter is "gifted." I explained that I was not quite sure what this meant in technical terms, except that it had something to do with IQ. Knowing about the inherent biases in IQ tests, however, I was quite anxious about any agreement to rely on those tests for her placement. Instead, I wanted the counselor and other school personnel to know about my daughter's unusually advanced perception of some things in the world—like race and human nature. I told the counselor some of the stories I have told in this book (the rainbow and the Martin Luther King stories), trying to persuade her that my daughter was insightful and probably would excel in the school's most challenging programs if she were given the chance. The counselor advised me that my daughter would be tested by the school psychologist to evaluate whether she belonged in the gifted class. It could be months into the school year before the psychologist evaluated her, however. To avoid this delay, I could have her tested privately, at my own expense. She encouraged me to do this, explained the qualifications criteria to me, and convinced me it would be advantageous for my daughter to start right away with the gifted class in the fall, if that was where she placed.

Following her advice, I arranged for my daughter to be evaluated in June. The placement test was a basic IQ test and a child needed a certain score to place into the gifted class. As the counselor explained to me, the school system set a lower qualifying score for Black children because they wanted to increase the number of Black children in the program. Given the racial bias against Blacks, as a group, on standard IQ tests, it seemed fair to use a different scoring system for children of color. The system also had a "teacher observation" questionnaire to evaluate certain skills of the child. Again, qualifying scores for Black children were different than they were for White. As was explained to me, the observation scores were used in close cases where the IQ score might not reflect the child's ability according to what the teacher had observed. In other words, if the child received an IQ score over the qualifying cut-off, then he or she, absent extenuating circumstances, would be placed in the program.

I understood the rules when I left the counselor's office. Thus, when my daughter achieved the requisite qualifying score on the "white" scale, I was confident she would be placed in the gifted program. In some ways, my daughter's score affirms the conclusion that the test is largely about exposure to information and less about native intelligence. Although Black, my daughter is being raised in a "White, middle-class" environment.

But it is not that easy and I need to add an important caveat. It is critical for Whites to understand that it would be impossible for any Black child, regardless of her socioeconomic class, to escape totally the bias of standardized exams. This is true because it is impossible for a Black child to see the world as a White child. To be Black necessarily is to interpret the world in a different way from the way a White child interprets it. Unlike the White child, the Black child struggles with the inner conflict created by notions like color-blindness and the subtle lessons that instill the precept of Black inferiority and White superiority in the Black child. Middle-class Black children, like my daughter, are not able to avoid this. Thus, any comparisons made between a White child's and a Black child's intelligence as measured by standardized exams must take these significant differences into account. Thus far, standardized exams have not been able to control for this critical difference, which makes a comparison of their exam results meaningless—*even if the children come from the same socioeconomic class.*

The score results were reported to her school and I thought we were set for the fall. A few days before class, however, the guidance counselor advised me that my daughter would not be placed in the program right away because she needed to be observed for six weeks by her teacher. I asked why this step was necessary and the counselor explained that the observation period was required because my daughter was coming from out of town. I didn't understand the reasoning and asked what the purpose of the observation period was. I wanted to know what the teacher would be looking for in my daughter and why the IQ score was not sufficient for placement purposes. I inquired whether her kindergarten teacher could fill out the observation form to expedite the process. Impossible, I was told; the observation had to be done by someone in the school district. Strictly a procedural step, she assured me.

"A procedural step!" I tried to advocate for my daughter, explaining how I had been told reliance was placed on the IQ score, which I did not like but knew I had to accept. I understood the observation score was not needed except in close cases. This is one reason I so willingly paid for the IQ testing myself so she could start right away with the correct placement. Even the guidance counselor had advised me to have the testing done because it would be better for her to start school in the appropriate class. We were both concerned that she not have to make a change from one class to another six weeks into the school year. Because I had not met my daughter's teacher, I also was concerned about her placement being dependent on one teacher's subjective observation, which presumably could override the IQ test score.

I felt bad for the guidance counselor as I saw her trying to solve my problem. I don't know why I had the expectation that she should and would be able to control my daughter's placement. I knew so well from my own experiences practicing law and teaching law that just because a woman holds a certain position in a law firm or on a faculty, it does not necessarily follow that she has power to help other women. To be in a position of true power, a person has to be fairly close to the top decision-making level of an organization. The source of power at the school was not the guidance counselor but the principal—a White woman.

So the guidance counselor and I went to the principal and put the burden on her to place my daughter in the gifted program at the beginning of the school year. In the presence of the guidance counselor, the principal assured me that my daughter's teacher would see the gifted qualities in my daughter and told me not to worry about my daughter's observation scores. But when I tried to explain that if all three of us were confident that my daughter would be placed into the program by "observation," why not give her the benefit of the doubt and go ahead and place her and observe her in the program, the principal emphatically stated that was impossible, because what if my daughter "really didn't belong in that class?" The trauma of being changed from that class back to the regular class would hurt her, the principal explained. I could not persuade the principal to see that her decision to delay my daughter's placement in the program guaranteed that my daughter would have to make a change at least six weeks into the program because we all knew she belonged in the most academically challenging class. Was it only co-incidental that there were no African Americans in the gifted class my daughter originally was scheduled to join?

With one phone call in mid-August, my daughter's certain place-ment in the program (since June) became uncertain. I questioned whether the school was sincerely interested in placing Black children in the gifted program. I wondered if even the "different scoring" system to account for the bias on the IQ test was a sham, designed to make it look like the school was doing its best to integrate the gifted program when, in fact, it really had no interest in achieving that goal. I did not express these concerns at the meeting, however, because I felt at the mercy of everyone involved in the placement decision.

Frustration again, made all the more intense because this time I had a Black professional working with me, also trying to get her boss to cross the color line and see the world from that perspective. *I still got nowhere.* The Black guidance counselor and I were both powerless to mediate across the color line and reach the White principal. While this was an-other new lesson in disappointment for me, I'm betting that the Black guidance counselor had learned this lesson many years before and expe-rienced it a zillion times over. I left school that morning feeling dejected but also taking some comfort in knowing that my daughter would not be targeted for a classroom that underestimated her abilities, consistent with national statistics. In this way, we beat some of the odds, although it momentarily crossed my mind that the observation could have been imposed on my daughter to see whether she really belonged in the spe-cial education class.

Admittedly, I was suspicious about the real reason for the dearth of

Black children in the school's gifted program; in some grades, there were no Black children in the gifted program. The admissions rules for the program seemed unnecessarily rigid and arbitrary, particularly in light of their effect on Black children. There was an obvious disconnect between the stated goal of integrating the gifted program and delaying the placement of a gifted Black child in the program with the possibility that the placement might not be made at all. I was on notice to pay careful attention to all the school's decisions about my daughter from that moment on. I was no longer just a mother; now I was a lawyer, too.

Hold on. I quickly learned how meaningless my lawyering skills were in dealing with my daughter's school. I was unsuccessful at getting her admitted to the gifted class at the beginning of the school year and was forced to wait out the six weeks. Fortunately, my daughter's teacher did see the "gifts" my daughter has and strongly recommended her for the program. I was relieved because my daughter had been asking constantly when she was going to be able to go with her friends to the "other" class. I felt confident in telling her it would happen any day now, because it was already late September, early October. Much to my dismay, however, I was told the paperwork had to be done before she could start attending the class.

By mid- to late-October, the paperwork was still pending. I pleaded with the principal and the guidance counselor to go ahead and place my daughter while the paperwork was pending. The principal told me she could not do that under any circumstances or she would lose funding for the school. I sat in her office in disbelief and imagined the following conversation:

Me: Do you really think if you place a Black child (with a high IQ and one who has been observed for six weeks by your own staff and strongly recommended for the program) into the gifted program pending completion of the paperwork that you will lose funding for the school? Wouldn't you be able to defend your decision?

Principal: I need to have the paperwork done because there have been occasions in the past when school officials in the district have placed children in inappropriate programs and the parents have gotten upset. So state law requires us to follow the rules.

Me: I can understand your concern with placing children erroneously. I agree that care should be taken to ensure that a child is not placed in an inappropriate program, especially if the program underestimates the child's ability. With respect to my daughter, all the testing indicates and we all agree she should be in the program and we are simply waiting for the paperwork. This is a correct placement. It is in her best interest to join the program as soon as possible so that she receives the academic challenge she needs. I can't imagine the superintendent's office admonishing you—and certainly not taking away your funding—for making this placement pending the paperwork. Furthermore, there are almost no Black children in the program and it is essential, consistent with your own goals, to integrate it. Here is a child who belongs in the program and you should not hesitate to put her there.

When I came out of my reverie, I asked the principal if she had discretionary powers to override rules when situations called for it, as this situation did. Again, she told me she did not have that kind of power. I wanted to ask her how she could stand doing her job if she had no discretionary power, if she had no moral compulsion to do right by the children. I could feel the anger building up inside me. Once again, I faced a situation of wanting to help my child and not wanting to have my advocacy backfire on her. The principal assured me the paperwork would be done within a few days.

A few days. Okay, we could wait a bit longer. Early November came, though, and still no placement. I called the School Board office and talked to a representative, hoping she would see how silly this situation had become. But she supported the principal, explaining that some parents had gotten upset because their children had been placed in the wrong classrooms based on the school officials' underestimating the children's abilities. To avoid more mistakes, officials were required to do everything by the book. I could not get the Board representative to see that my daughter's placement was correct, based on all the testing and observations; that I wanted my daughter in the program; and that it would be in my daughter's best interest to be in the program as soon as possible.

I asked if there was anything I could do to expedite this process. She advised me that I could request a formal hearing and so I did. But as soon as I made the request, she got perturbed with me. "Don't you know someone from (the state capital) would have to come down here and evaluate your daughter and it would be very formal?" What she really meant was that formal hearings are a big burden to school board personnel. I replied, "If we were to have a formal hearing, what do you think the hearing officer will tell the school to do?" She said, matter-of-factly and condescendingly, "They'll probably tell the school to put your daughter in the gifted class." "Exactly," I exclaimed. "So I want a formal hearing, if that's what it takes to get things done." She sighed and said, "Okay. We'll be in touch."

Within a few days, the principal's secretary called me. Miraculously, the paperwork had been completed, obviating the need for a formal hearing. Before the placement, however, I was required to meet with the principal, the gifted teacher, and the guidance counselor to discuss the educational plan for my daughter. The secretary suggested we meet on a day that I had to be out of town to give a talk at another law school. I couldn't cancel that obligation, which had been arranged for months. The secretary then told me that the meeting would have to wait another two weeks because the principal wouldn't be available again until then. I suggested that we go ahead and place my daughter in the class and meet in a few weeks. The secretary told me that would be impossible; the meetings were a necessary prerequisite to the placement. I told her I wanted to waive my right to the preplacement meeting. She told me I could not. My laughter broke the momentum of this tit-for-tat conversation. It wasn't that I thought the situation was funny; rather, my laughter reflected my exasperation. I replied to the secretary, "Do you know that a person who is accused of murder in our criminal justice system can waive his right to an attorney, he can plead guilty to the charge, he can even ask for the death penalty? Doesn't it seem ironic and silly that I cannot waive my right to this meeting? Think about it. The principal, guidance counselor, and I have met several times on this issue. We've been meeting for over six months, for heaven's sake! And I've already met the gifted teacher, too." (I had gone to her directly and asked for her help in placing my daughter but was cavalierly brushed off with the comment that every parent thinks her child is gifted.)

The poor secretary must have thought I was crazy because all the frustration that had been building up was finally coming out in this hysteria at her. I calmed down, apologized, and assured her that I knew this wasn't her fault. Calmly and politely, I asked, "Would you please tell the principal, the guidance counselor, and the gifted teacher that I want my daughter placed in the program tomorrow. If anyone wants to call me, I'd be happy to talk. But I will bring my daughter to school tomorrow and personally accompany her to the gifted classroom." She meekly said, "Okay."

Later that evening, I thought about the tremendous gains America has made in terms of promoting racial equality. But I also realized that in some ways, little has changed from the days when America had to desegregate its public schools. In those days, Black children had to be accompanied to the White schools by federal officials who were responsible for ensuring their safety and protecting their rights to be in the school. The next day, I was going to accompany my daughter to her school, too. Although her physical safety wasn't my concern and no one was trying to keep her out of the school, I was concerned about protecting her psychological well-being and I also needed to protect her right to be in the gifted class within the school. Many integrated public schools still maintain segregated classrooms on the inside and this is most notable in the three-tier tracking system.

At our fifteen-minute meeting the next day, the teacher of the gifted class coldly greeted me and informed me that my daughter had placed into her class. She said this as if this were startling news, like I was supposed to say, "What a wonderful surprise!" I sat in my teeny-tiny chair at a teeny-tiny table in the classroom and looked at her cross-eyed with disbelief. The guidance counselor did not look at me (and the principal could not make the meeting). The teacher explained a little bit about the program and then asked me if I wanted my daughter to join the group. She honestly did all this with no affect whatsoever; she merely described the projects the children would be working on the rest of the school year (now half over) and informed me there would be extra fees, which I could pay then if I wanted to. I didn't know if her bland presentation was supposed to cause me to be disinterested in the program, and perhaps she wanted me to say, "No. I'm sorry. This sounds dreadfully boring and your program just isn't right for my daughter." Given all that we had been through, she may have been surprised that I enthusiastically responded, telling her how excited my daughter was, relating that my daughter and I had heard so many good things about her class, and offering to volunteer if she needed any help.

Just before Thanksgiving my daughter started the class. I had been worried she would have to make a change six weeks into the school year, and now the school year was almost half over. She made the change relatively smoothly, but I was angry at the school officials for putting her, the only Black girl selected from her class for participation in the program, in the position of bearing the burden of the change so late into the school year. I was shocked that no one wanted to advocate for her with me. No one assumed a leadership role on her behalf. I feared I had no goodwill at my daughter's school anymore.

After contending with the school officials' resistance to my daughter's placement in the gifted program for most of the fall semester, I was hoping no other incidents would occur concerning my daughter. After my daughter's placement in the gifted class, then, I tried to stay out of "trouble" and keep a low profile, quietly playing out the "ordinary" parent role of bringing snacks and doing whatever else the teacher asked me to do.

I cannot "prove" that the school officials discriminated against my daughter or that they generally disfavored the placement of children of color in the gifted program. During the process, however, I learned of one White second-grade boy who was placed in a gifted class in one of the county's schools in August, although he also came from out of state. When I asked how he could be placed without being observed by his teacher for six weeks, I was told it was because he had been in a gifted class in first grade in the other state and so there was no need to observe him. In my daughter's case, she needed to be observed because she was starting school and an evaluation of my daughter's ability from her out-of-state kindergarten teacher was not sufficient to meet the policy's requirement. This made no sense to me. The in-state observation requirement for my daughter but not for the boy, coupled with the virtual exclusion of Black children from the gifted programs county-wide, inspired me to ask for the statistical breakdown by race and sex on the placement of children in the gifted class in the county. However, I was told the data was unavailable.

My purpose in telling this story is to share the frustration I experienced and the unfair way I think my daughter's placement decision was made and to point out the relevancy of my daughter's race in that decision. Obviously, the school officials were conscious of her race, yet they did nothing to facilitate her placement and carry through on their publicly stated goal of integrating the gifted class. It is quite telling that no one ever said they were sorry for the delay in her placement or for imposing all the nonsensical requirements. The principal avoided me and never called me or met with me after the decision was made. Notice how cold the gifted teacher was—our meeting was very perfunctory. The overwhelming message they gave me was that my daughter may have gotten the right to be in the gifted program, but they were not happy about it. Even the guidance counselor's silence was revealing. Both she and my daughter were breaking barriers at the school, apparently to the dismay of some White officials. Rather than being comforted that my daughter was in the gifted class and that school personnel would know she is bright, I became worried that school personnel might mistreat her because they weren't convinced she really belonged in the class. In other words, the struggle to get her into the class was just that: a struggle. It was not a cooperative, joint effort with concerned educators; it was a lonely parental struggle. Consequently, it crossed my mind that the officials and teachers might resent me for pushing to get my daughter into the program and I worried that they might take their resentment out on my daughter. My worry was not unfounded.

THE DINOSAUR EXHIBIT

Shortly after joining the gifted class, my daughter started her first project, which was to write a report on a dinosaur of her choice. The class was working toward the goal of having a dinosaur display in the classroom for all their parents and other students in the school to visit. On "Dinosaur Day," the children would be stationed around the room, available to answer any questions about their dinosaurs.

My daughter did all the research on her dinosaur and wrote the report herself. The children also were encouraged to draw a picture of their dinosaur or make a clay model of it. My daughter elected to make a clay model of hers and spent hours working on it. She anticipated Dinosaur Day with great enthusiasm. It was going to be an extra special day because her grandparents were visiting and were going to come with me to the class. I had my camera and planned to take lots of pictures for our album.

The classroom was divided by a science lab-desk for use by the teacher. The lab-desk was situated approximately three feet in front of the blackboard, was about four feet tall, and ran pretty much the width of the room. The children's tables were placed on the other side of the desk. As my parents and I entered my daughter's classroom, I was utterly shocked and outraged at what I saw. All of the children except my daughter and one little White girl were situated at the tables in front of the lab-desk. The other little girl was along the same wall as my daughter, right inside the door as you entered the room. Down the wall, easily ten feet from her, next to the storage closet and behind the lab desk, was my daughter. It was as if my daughter were not supposed to be a part of the class. The only Black child in the class was stuck off in the corner, behind a desk she could not see over and no one could see her behind it.

I quietly asked my parents to go stay with my daughter while I talked with her teacher. Once again, I thought, "Oh no, here I go complaining again, that's what she is going to think." But I had to say something because my daughter had virtually been excluded from participating in a meaningful, equal way with her classmates in the dinosaur exhibit. If my parents or I strayed away from her to engage with the other children, she would have been left alone in the corner. In essence, then, we had all been relegated to the corner.

I asked the teacher if I could speak with her privately and we stepped to the side of the students and visitors. I wanted to know if there had been a discipline problem with my daughter that had caused the teacher to put my daughter practically in the closet. Even if that had been the case, I would not have condoned what the teacher did. On the other hand, I wanted to give the teacher the benefit of the doubt; perhaps she felt justified in segregating my daughter from her classmates. The teacher responded that she just did not have enough room in the classroom for all the students on the same side of the desk.

Her response was disingenuous. First, there were only eight or nine students in the class and the classroom was designed for a regular-size class. More telling of the teacher's motivation was her response when I suggested that what she had done to my daughter was cruel. I did not use this word lightly; it *was* cruel to isolate one child from her classmates and I believed that *anyone* should be able to see this but placed an especially high burden on a *teacher* to see the effects of her decision. Continuing, I also told the teacher that what she had done was racist. Again, I did not use this word lightly, either; whether it was conscious or unconscious, it *was* racist for the teacher to put the only Black child in the class off in the corner where no one could see her.

Admittedly, I was harsh with the teacher and more direct than I had ever been with a school official, notwithstanding all that my daughter and I had been through trying to get her into this very class. I was visibly upset. I am sure I had an angry expression on my face; my whole demeanor probably conveyed my profound anger at the teacher. Given how upset I was, the teacher's response was inappropriate and only made me angrier.

Defensively, she said she had not even noticed that no one could see my daughter behind the desk. She said she hadn't even realized she'd picked the only Black child in the class to stand behind the desk. She quickly added that the other little White girl was also on that same wall.

I interpreted the teacher's response as a sign that she thought that I was overreacting; that my sense of outrage at her insensitivity was unfounded. But I was justifiably upset and I pointed out to the teacher that everyone who came through the door was interacting with the White girl who was on the same wall as my daughter. The White girl, then, was not excluded at all. In contrast, no one was interacting with my daughter because no one could even see her.

The teacher became upset, perhaps realizing that I was getting even angrier. She tried to justify her decision by repeating that she did not have enough room for all the children to be on one side of the lab-desk. She started talking nonstop, giving me no chance to respond to what she was saying. Finally, she asked in exasperation, "What am I supposed to do? What do you want me to do? Do you want me to move her?"

The situation was not bringing out the best in me and I was getting embarrassed that other parents and students might be watching us. I could see my parents and my daughter off in the corner by themselves, my parents engaging their granddaughter in conversation, undoubtedly to distract her. Naturally, I wanted the teacher to move my daughter to the other side of the desk, but I didn't want to make this decision for her and let her off so easily. I responded somewhat indignantly, "I want to see you use your best judgment." The teacher went over to my daughter and asked her if she wanted to move around the lab-desk to be with the other children. My daughter was so happy and quickly agreed to that. Other parents then immediately engaged her in conversations about her dinosaur. It made a huge difference for my daughter to be on the side of the desk with all of her classmates. When I asked about moving the other little White girl, too, the teacher told me she was against that wall because she had a cold and the teacher didn't want to expose the other students to it. The teacher said she was okay because everyone could see her as they came through the door. And this was true; everyone was interacting with her, which made me wonder how many of us would catch her cold anyway so why not move her? But I did not pursue it; fighting for my daughter left me exhausted.

When my parents and I returned home, my father said, "Well, I guess they still have segregation here in the South. What was her teacher thinking about, treating her that way?" My father is from Alabama and knows all too well what Jim Crow was like. He also is very temperate and judicious, as is my mother. They vented their anger for days after this, calling my sisters and relating how awful it was.

That evening after my daughter was asleep, I talked to my parents because I wanted to know their perceptions of the incident and I wanted to explain why the teacher's decision to isolate my daughter was so disturbing. I was concerned with the message the isolation gave to both my daughter and everyone else in the room that day. My daughter was being told that she was unworthy to participate in the class in the same way as her White classmates. And why? My daughter could have reached only one conclusion: The teacher put her in the corner because she is Black. The teacher's decision undermined my daughter's confidence and damaged her self-esteem.

Significantly, the teacher also gave everyone else in the room that day the message of my daughter's inferiority and the concomitant message of everyone else's superiority. The only visible distinction between my daughter and everyone else was race. Thus, the teacher's decision to isolate my daughter sent a resounding message of Black inferiority and White superiority reverberating throughout the room. The White students and parents were being taught by the gifted teacher that Blacks do not belong in her classroom. She may not have consciously thought this was what she was doing, but on some level, she must have known she was hurting my daughter. She may have been telling me, "Well, you can fight to get your daughter into my class, but that doesn't mean I have to treat her like she's really in my class."

I commented to my parents that one of the most telling things about the gifted teacher and one of the things that caused me the most concern was that she never seemed remorseful; she never said, "Oh, I'm sorry. I didn't realize what I had done and of course, you're right. We'll move her right away." Quite the contrary. She got defensive and turned the problem around on me and asked me to solve it for her. The scary part of this is that she knew my parents and I were coming to school that day. She knew we would see how she was treating my daughter, but then maybe that was the point. The teacher knew how upset I would be. I wondered if the teacher always treated my daughter this disrespectfully.

I wanted to tell the principal about it but realized she was unlikely to be sympathetic after all we had been through. I had nowhere to go with this injustice to make it right. I started thinking about private school, a last resort because private schools have very few children of color attending them. What was better for my daughter: This? Or a private school? I wondered.

Over the next few days, I calmed down and reflected on the incident. The one arguably "good" thing that came out of this was for my parents to witness the unjust way their granddaughter had been treated. I tell them about unfair incidents that happen to my daughter and they are very supportive. But this time it happened to them, too. The racism hurt them directly because no one wants their loved ones to hurt. I think that watching this incident helped my parents understand in a different, much deeper way what their granddaughter goes through on a daily basis. Although I do not wish for my parents or anyone to hurt, when White people *feel* some of the pain of racism, I believe that they become stronger allies in the struggle for racial equality. I wish we had more allies.

I will never forget the scene in my child's room that day. It was ugly! Discrimination is ugly and my heart ached for my daughter and all the children of color in this world.

As time went by, the teacher and I kept a safe distance from each other. She became a bit meeker in her demeanor and I quietly participated as a parent in the classroom activities. Meanwhile, my daughter enjoyed certain aspects of the program; it was considerably more challenging and interesting than her "regular" class. For example, the class dissected fetal pigs one week. I visited my daughter's class one of the days that week and the smell of formaldehyde was enough to make me sick, but I have to admit, it was fascinating. The children had learned all about anatomy and approached the project with considerable preparedness. Yet I wondered why this opportunity was not available to all the students. Parents had paid for their child's pig, and I'm sure parents of children who were not in the gifted class would have willingly paid, as well. If a parent could not afford it, which may have been the case even among the tracked gifted group, then other arrangements could have been made. I am convinced that every child could have learned immensely from the fetal pig dissection experience and I was sorry that only a select group got to do it.

As I watched my daughter and the other children in the class flourish with curiosity dissecting the fetal pigs, I remained concerned that all of her Black classmates and some of her White classmates were not allowed to join in the intellectual experiences she was having. My concern reached its peak, however, with the end-of-the-year celebrations at the school. Customarily, the children in all the gifted classes are taken on a field trip to an educational amusement park. The teacher uses the excursion to reward the students for their hard work all year long and also to teach them about other cultures around the world. Parents are required to pay an extra fee for this trip. Understandably, there is a tremendous amount of fanfare and hoopla surrounding the adventure.

Yet the joy, excitement, and anticipation of the students going on the trip are probably no match for the sorrow, jealousy, and hurt the students who are not going on the trip must feel. As the students from the gifted class—almost all of whom are White—are off on their exciting adventure, the students who are literally left behind—almost all the Black children—are taken on a local field trip that pales in comparison. For example, one year the students were taken to the local Burger King for their end-of-the-year-celebration.

The field trips had nothing to do with academic abilities and conveyed social messages about the worth of the children. If everyone had gone on the same field trip, all of the children would have been exposed to different and valuable aspects of life. Dividing the children into academic groups—which had dramatic racial and economic implications as well—exploited the advantage that White, economically privileged children have over Black children and economically underprivileged children. The field trips heightened the already all-too-familiar division between the children.

My daughter may be an exception to the general rule that most "gifted" students are White, but I don't want her to learn it is okay to devalue people the way the "regular" students were devalued at her school. There simply was no sound educational reason for such dramatically different kinds of field trips for the two groups of students. All the children deserved better mentoring. All the children of color deserved better, period!

THE DEVELOPMENTAL LAB SCHOOL: HIGH HOPES

Fortunately, that summer I received news that my daughter had been admitted off the waiting list into the university's developmental laboratory school. I was happy to take her out of the first school, partly because the school was not sincerely interested in her achievement, but also because of the way I saw the "regular" children treated. Disastrous Dinosaur Day also provided added incentive to move to another school. At the developmental lab school, I expected my daughter to be treated with dignity and to be appreciated because of her race. The school population reflected the population in the county based on race, sex, and socioeconomic class. This, coupled with the fact that the school was administered by the education department at the university, seemed to make it an ideal setting. I believed it had to be better for my daughter than the school that devalued her.

Students at the developmental lab school benefited from their affiliation with the university. For example, classrooms were staffed with an unusually high number of adults at various times over the year because the teachers had aides and they also occasionally had graduate students pursuing advanced degrees, doing research and working with the children. It was a unique environment in terms of the adult-contact hours the children enjoyed.

One month before the end of my daughter's first year at the school, I was talking with a teacher after I dropped my daughter off in the morning. As we were chatting, another woman joined us, who was introduced to me as the school's gifted teacher. I responded, "Oh, I didn't know the school had a gifted program. That's odd that no one would mention it to me because my daughter was in the gifted program in her previous school. I noted that in her chart and because no one said anything to me about it, I assumed the idea of a gifted class was at odds with the idea of a developmental lab school. So I didn't pursue it."

The gifted teacher warmly responded, "Oh, if your daughter was in the gifted program at her previous school, she definitely should be in it here. I'll check her file and get right back to you."

I immediately made an appointment to talk with the regular classroom teacher, a White woman, so I could hear firsthand why this mistake had occurred. At our meeting, I explained my concern that she had not recommended my daughter for the gifted class. She responded, "I checked Mary's file and sure enough, can you believe it, her IQ is [over the qualifying number]. We'll place her in the class right away."

I appreciated that I wasn't going to have to fight the system again, which was an enormous relief. Everyone immediately acknowledged their mistake and worked to correct it. Nevertheless, the teacher's response and her cavalier tone were insulting. *"Can you believe it?"* she had the nerve to ask me? Did she think I was going to respond with something like, "Yes, it's hard to believe, isn't it? A bright Black child," or something like that? Was her disbelief at the accuracy of my daughter's IQ an invitation for me to confirm her suspicions, become a coconspirator in affirming a stereotype she had about Blacks? Was she unable to grasp that I was the child's mother? What parent would ever betray her child the way she was asking me to? What made her think I would do such a thing? The answer was obvious: She thought our shared Whiteness would (should?) override my motherly love and cause me momentarily to disown my daughter and affirm the teacher's mistaken judgment.

Clearly, the teacher did not think my daughter belonged in the gifted class, but, to her dismay, the IQ numbers spoke for themselves. If this teacher had been responsible for observing my daughter for possible placement in the gifted class, she would not have recommended my daughter. After all, the teacher had a whole year with my daughter and she never saw my daughter's "gifts" or recommended her for the gifted class.

I mustered up my courage and said something like this to the teacher: "I am concerned that almost a whole year has gone by and that neither you nor any of the other teachers or graduate students affiliated with this class could see that my daughter is especially bright. I'm left to conclude one of two things: You and your staff did not bring out the best in my daughter, or you didn't expect her to be bright because she is Black and she fit a stereotype you believe in."

As I said these last words, I'm sure I didn't take a breath, I was so nervous. I don't enjoy being put in awkward positions where I'm forced to offend or hurt people. A person who is defensive is less likely to learn from situations. I had to say something to impress on my daughter's teacher how damaging her low expectations of my daughter (all Black children?) were. She had a lot to say in how my daughter is perceived by others in the school community. Critically, the teacher also had enormous influence over my daughter and my daughter learned from her how much self-respect she should give herself. Any teacher plays a significant role in shaping a child's self-esteem. If a teacher cannot bring out the best in a child, then the child won't act, think, or feel at her best. How was I to measure the harm the teacher's casual attitude about my daughter's abilities caused?

To her credit, the teacher responded sympathetically. "I can understand that you are upset. We should have screened your daughter when she first joined the school. It's right in her record and we should have seen it. I can't explain why it was overlooked. And your daughter is so quiet that I didn't notice it. Most gifted students draw attention to themselves and your daughter didn't."

"Yes, she is a quiet little girl, but I don't understand why every child is not screened for proper placement because not all children demand attention. Maybe there are other 'gifted' quiet children in the class, too. Moreover, if you had taken the time to know my daughter, you would have seen the wonderful ways she looks at the world. I'm sorry you didn't do that. I am going to talk with the principal about this to make sure it doesn't happen to other children. I hope you understand."

In my meeting with the principal, I expressed my concerns that none of the teachers, aides, or graduate students bothered to know my daughter well enough to see her talents. How could she have gotten so little attention? I asked how many children of color were in the gifted program at the school and was told that the school only keeps "pencil" statistics on that kind of data, but they hoped to have it all computerized in the near future. The principal assured me, however, that her program was one of the most racially diverse in the county. I believed her but was not persuaded that being "one of the most racially diverse programs" meant much of anything. My daughter's placement in the lab school's program, for example, meant that her gifted class now had *one* Black girl in it. This was the same statistic as at her previous school, and, ironically, my daughter was the statistic.

The situation at the developmental lab school merely reinforced my feelings that school officials at both schools were color-conscious but in ways that worked to the detriment of my daughter. Again, I cannot prove it, but is it coincidental that her placement in the gifted class at both schools took so long? At the first school, officials knew she was gifted and dragged their feet in the placement process. At the lab school, school officials ignored the information I gave them (in writing and orally) about my daughter's gifted placement in the prior school, they never mentioned their own gifted program to me, no one ever recommended my daughter be evaluated for the program the entire year, and when their neglect of my daughter became evident, they cavalierly dismissed their mistake as an oversight. My daughter did not get the attention she needed from her teachers. Again, is it coincidental that she was the only Black girl to successfully place into the gifted program in her grade in both schools?

These placement stories about my daughter are disturbing, but they border on tragic when I stop to reflect on how hard it is for *all* Black children to beat the odds that they will suffer race discrimination in their school-placement decisions. Many parents do not have time to go to their child's school over and over again, reminding school officials of their particular problems. Many parents are uncomfortable (for any number of reasons) about approaching school officials to discuss seemingly unfair situations with respect to their children. These stories are important, then, not because they prove anything in an absolute way, but rather because they offer some evidence of the racism—conscious and unconscious—in one public school district. They illustrate how difficult it is to overcome institutional barriers to racial equality. These struggles remind me as the White mother of a Black child that my lawyering ability is virtually useless in trying to overcome racial inequality—even if I focus on just one little girl.

As the White mother of a Black child, I confront White adults more and more frequently as I try to protect my daughter. I have learned that the distance across the color line is too great for most White people. As long as this huge gap exists between White America and Black America, parents of Black children will be put in confrontational positions with their children's White teachers. If there is any environment where the racial gap can and should be eliminated, it is in our public schools.

4

RACIAL CHALLENGES
Overcoming Fear of Differences

ON THIEVES, POODLES, AND THE KKK

Racial differences pose a challenge for many people for a variety of reasons. For example, many Whites will admit they are afraid of Blacks because a common, predominant image Whites have of Blacks is that of the violent criminal. Moreover, being Black challenges my daughter, who sometimes feels anxious about how she will be treated by Whites. Finally, I admit that raising a Black child is more challenging than I imagined. Some days, I wish I could pull the covers over my head and sleep through the "what's-going-to-happen-to-her-today incident." She once said to me that she wanted to wear a miniature video camera so I could "see what it's like at school. Then you'd know what I have to put up with." As her mother, I am her primary guardian—the one person she is supposed to be able to count on to protect her and keep her safe from harm. Each morning, I open her bedroom curtains to the bright sunshine, giving her a similar sunny good morning kiss and hug. I approach each day genuinely hoping it will be a good one for her and that however the day's racism decides to evidence itself will be only "mildly" hurtful. Some days are better than others on the racism barometer.

WHY ARE SOME WHITES SCARED OF BLACKS— EVEN A LITTLE BLACK GIRL?

My daughter was six years old and we were on our way to New Hampshire to climb her first mountain on Friday, October 13, 1995.[31]

As we were waiting for our connecting flight in Logan International Airport in Boston, she was off exploring the waiting lounge and getting drinks of water—all within my sight, of course. A White woman sat down next to me and placed her luggage in front of her chair. She hadn't been sitting long when her connecting flight was called. As she gathered her belongings, she noticed her purse was missing. I helped her look around the immediate area for it but did not see it. We looked around perhaps ten seconds; it did not take long to see it was not there, when she loudly announced, "I bet that Black kid took it." She was pointing directly at my daughter, the only child and the only Black person in the waiting area.

If the woman had reflected for a moment before making her accusation, she would have realized how silly her conclusion was. My daughter certainly was not trying to make a getaway; she was doing ballet turns in the waiting area, oblivious to everyone around her, and clearly did not have possession of a purse. I was so stunned and offended by the woman's accusation, though, that I could not point this out to her. Instead, I responded, "I'm sorry, but you are talking about my daughter and I can assure you she is not a thief. Perhaps you left your purse at the ticket counter." Sure enough, she returned from the counter with her purse and flew out the door, remarking as she went, "Well, it's Friday the 13th. What do you expect?"

I was momentarily dumbstruck. I wasn't sure what I expected. Clearly, I did not expect an adult White woman to be suspicious of a six-year-old child—Black or White, girl or boy—doing ballet twirls in the waiting area of an airport. I did not expect my daughter to pose a threat to her. How long had the woman been "on guard," watching my daughter, afraid my daughter might hurt her or rob her? The racism behind the woman's fear was readily apparent by her public accusation. Perhaps she realized this, too, which is why she tried to blame her behavior on the fact that it was Friday the 13th—if that makes any sense to anyone. Perhaps I was supposed to be forgiving of her racism because it was an unlucky day, especially for her. What bad luck that she made her comment to me, not realizing I was the accused thief's mother. On a luckier day, perhaps some other Whites would have joined with her in her racist conspiracy. To her "unlucky" fortune, now those of us in the waiting area, perfect strangers, knew her "secret" feelings about Blacks and if this information were known to people she knew, she might be embarrassed. Her unconscious racism bubbled to the surface and, embarrassingly, an innocent six-year-old girl was the victim. Pretty scary for a goodwill White to stoop this low. Maybe it was embarrassing enough that a few people learned about her true feelings and that was her bad luck for the day. To be honest, I did not understand what she meant by associating her comment with Friday the 13th. From my daughter's perspective, Friday the 13th was no different from any other day when it comes to assumptions some Whites have about her based on her race.

Certainly, I had never, ever imagined that my daughter would be accused of stealing. I realize the stereotype of the Black man as a criminal is rampant in our society, as I discuss in chapter 7. But my daughter was both the wrong sex and the wrong age to fit this stereotype. Most important, if I had an older Black son and this had happened to him, the accusation still would have shaken me to the core. I simply did not expect to be emotionally assaulted by a stranger in the airport making such an ugly accusation about my child.

My daughter did not hear the woman's accusation, but she will learn about it when she reads this book. I hope when that day comes that she will be sufficiently older and will be able to situate the racist thinking behind the accusation in the White woman and not internalize it as a message about Black inferiority. The woman's accusation was outrageous, but it was only one of many ways in which my daughter is rebuffed by White society every day. The White woman in the airport is not alone in her fear of Blacks, even little Black girls. I remember when my daughter was less than two years old and we were walking in the neighborhood park. My daughter spotted a White woman who was walking her poodle (which was also white) and ran toward it, hoping to be able to pet the dog. The woman saw my daughter running her way and immediately snatched the poodle up in her arms and walked away. My daughter turned and looked at me for an explanation.

I remember thinking, "Why is this woman afraid of my daughter?" I tried to rationalize her reaction to my daughter. Perhaps the woman did not want her poodle around little children; perhaps the poodle had a mean disposition and the woman was actually protecting my daughter. I would have been open to these or other explanations if the woman had been friendly. Instead, she sneered at us, coddled her dog as if to protect it from my daughter, reversed course, and walked away. My daughter looked bewildered by the woman's actions and, at the time, I was at a loss to explain them. I remember the contrast in colors between my daughter and the poodle was vividly striking and I wonder if it struck the poodle's owner as well. Did she perceive my daughter as "impure," consistent with the beliefs of many Whites about Blacks? This thought crossed my mind, admittedly, without any concrete evidence that this was, in fact, what motivated the woman's behavior. A fleeting thought, but only temporarily, as the next incident unfolded within minutes.

As the woman and her poodle walked away, a swing caught my daughter's eye and she was off to enjoy it. It was a tire swing, which can easily hold a number of small children. As I helped my daughter onto the swing, a young White girl, perhaps six or seven, started running quickly toward the swing to join us. Amazingly, the girl's mother, who was also White, ran after her and literally picked her up before she reached the swing. This abrupt interruption of the girls' "game plan" caused them both to burst into tears as the young girl was carried off by her mother.

Like most Whites, I simply didn't want to believe or simply couldn't believe that race was relevant to these types of situations. It made me too uncomfortable. I tried to rationalize what had happened and come up with some reasons unrelated to race for the women's behavior. The mother and daughter may have been in a hurry and had no time to play, I thought. But this made little sense because they had just arrived at the park. On the other hand, it may have been coincidental that the two White women shunned my daughter within minutes of each other. Just because there was no friendly exchange between us but rather this dramatic avoidance of us doesn't mean they are afraid of Blackness, I told myself.

Gradually, over the years, I have become persuaded that my daughter's Blackness prevents some Whites from interacting with her. Why else would this story play itself out over and over again? For example, when my daughter was six, we went to a park with her huge red ball that was almost bigger than she was. Immediately, other children were attracted to it. It did not take long at all before a group of young Black children joined her in playing with the ball. I sat close to her on a swing, watching their interactions. It amazes me that children need no introductions; their youth alone is a sufficient invitation to friendship.

After twenty minutes or so, the Black children were called by their caretaker and left. My daughter played with the ball by herself for awhile, but I could see a group of young White children spying on her from behind a big oak tree. They seemed interested in playing with the ball, but they did not approach my daughter and, instead, ran off to some other attraction on the playground.

A White friend who was sitting on the swing with me remarked how odd it was that the Black children played with my daughter and the White children did not. I was relieved by my friend's comment, because I had told my White friends about some of the things that have happened to my daughter, but my stories may have seemed exaggerated or unbelievable. Sometimes they seem unbelievable to me, too, and I witness them. My friend's observation was affirming. I almost said, "You should live with us for a week and you'll see racism from a completely different perspective." Instead, I replied, "It's sad, isn't it? And I see this happen to her too many times. Let's go ask her if she wants to get some ice cream and head home."

Admittedly, I will never know with absolute certainty what motivated the poodle owner, the White mother, or the White children on the playground to keep a safe distance from my daughter. Over the years, however, I am convinced such incidents are race-related, and not just because they keep happening to my daughter. My subsequent studies have uncovered many similar stories related by Black folks. For example, in their 1994 book *Living with Racism,* Professors Joe Feagin and Melvin Sikes devote a whole section of their book to similar stories told by Blacks.[32] Having witnessed my daughter's stories, these other tales reinforce my conclusions.

Moreover, the relatedness of race to such incidents becomes clear if the focus shifts from the actor's state of consciousness to the observer's interpretation of the events. Assuming the mother who did not let her daughter play with mine on the swing was a person of goodwill, she did not intend to give her daughter any message about race by snatching her daughter up in front of mine. Remember, however, that racism often operates on us in unconscious ways. The poodle owner and the White children in the park also may have meant no racial harm by their behavior. Nevertheless, my daughter sees the relevance of race to these situations. Race is not something that gets buried in her unconscious or semiconscious state of mind. Ironically, when White people of goodwill put race out of their minds, they act in hurtful and insensitive ways that make race foremost in the minds of Blacks. That evening when we got home from the park where my daughter had played with the big red ball, she asked me why "those kids" wouldn't play with her. "Don't they know everyone can get hurt feelings even if they aren't White? I have a heart with feelings, too!" I bit my lip.

Significantly, other witnesses to these events also could interpret them as subtle (or not so subtle) messages that Whites should avoid interacting with Blacks. This may be more likely to result with respect to children who see these things happen. Young children who are learning about life and their environment are acutely sensitive to things around them. If my daughter reached the conclusion that race was relevant to the situations, it is likely that other children did as well. Consciously or unconsciously, children of color internalize the message of their racial inferiority and White children internalize the message of White superiority when these types of lessons are presented to them.

Moreover, even if the mother in the swing story tried to ameliorate the racial effects of her actions by justifying them to her daughter on other than race grounds at a later time, I had no other explanation to offer my daughter without making something up. Unlike the mother who may have had incentive to offer alternative rationales for her behavior precisely to keep her daughter from thinking she was racist (some evidence of her consciousness level), I have no incentive to keep the truth from my daughter. In fact, as my daughter gets older and matures, my responsibility to help her cope with racism grows.

When a very young Black child wants to teach White children that she and other Black children can get hurt feelings because they also have hearts, I know the racism is beginning to settle into her psyche and my motherly role as great protector gets shaken. Responsible, loving adults have a special obligation to teach children not to be racist. My experiences tell me that this goal can be achieved only if adults accept the challenge to overcome their fear of racial differences and talk positively about race to children.

LIVING WITH RACISM IS SCARY, TOO,
ESPECIALLY IF YOU ARE LITTLE

Occasionally, my daughter expresses her fears about being Black. Sometimes her apprehension and anxiety come out in subtle ways. We may be invited to an event and she will ask if there will be other Black people there. She usually asks if there will be other children there, too. Having other Black people and children at social events helps her feel comfortable about herself; she does not have to stand out because of her Blackness or her youth. Unfortunately, there are times when she is the only person of color or only child in a group and I often wonder how this makes her feel. Once, I took her with me to the welcoming reception for the African American students who had been accepted into the law school and she was the only child in attendance. Still, I thought it would be a positive experience for her. I realized she was somewhat uncomfortable, however, when I asked her if she wanted to wander around the room with me and meet some of the new people. She replied, "Oh, no, thank you. That won't be necessary. I know enough people." I laughed, but before I could respond, a few students who heard her turned around and said, "But you don't know us." They introduced themselves and my daughter was delighted with the attention.

One of the most difficult situations I have faced with my daughter and trying to explain racial animosity to her came one evening after we watched the news, one of my rituals that she has grown to respect even though it makes me one of the most boring people in her eyes. On this particular evening, there was a segment about the Ku Klux Klan, including footage of Klan members in their traditional regalia rallying around a burning cross. The segment came on the screen without any warning and was over almost as quickly. I was not even sure if she had seen it and I hoped the story had been just as uninteresting as the prior story depicting the Senate chambers where there was talk about some pending legislation. As I put her to bed that night, though, I knew she had seen the story about the KKK.

"Mom, who were those guys in the sheets?" she asked. "What were they doing?" I was not sure how much I should try to explain to a six-year-old, especially just before bedtime when nightmares might not be far off. On the other hand, I did not want to ignore or downplay the significance of her curiosity. I wanted to say to her, "Just a second," as I ran to the shelf and pulled off a parent's guidebook on how to explain the KKK to your Black child. Stalling, trying to pull my thoughts together, another part of me just wanted to hold her and rock her in my arms as I tried to get my silent tears under control so I could try to explain the inexplicable.

"People who dress like that belong to a club," I answered. Not such a good response, I thought. She thinks clubs are benign like the Chess Club at her school and the club in Little Rascals. When she responded, "Are they a bad club?" I asked her what she meant. I thought I would try to get her to talk so I could understand better what she already knew and what she was trying to find out. She had learned from somewhere that "those guys" kill Black people. I asked her where she learned that. Naively, I had always thought she would learn about things like the KKK from me, when I thought she was ready. She said, "I don't know. But why do they do that? Do they kill Black kids, too? Are they going to kill me? What if they see me walking? Are they in the park?" I thought her questions would never end. Seeing the KKK on the news brought some reality to a story she had learned before, but she was not sure whether the KKK actually existed. Now the truth was out and she was petrified that the KKK was going to get her.

I did not know where to begin in trying to explain the KKK to her. I wanted to be honest with her, but I also wanted to allay her fears that the KKK would get her. Lots of thoughts were going through my mind. The conversation reminded me of the time I joined in the march on Forsyth County, Georgia, in the late 1980s to protest its exclusion of Blacks. I rode to Atlanta where NAACP organizers had arranged for a bus convoy for the drive to Forsyth County. On the bus were many elderly Black men, some of whom had participated with Martin Luther King in the march from Selma to Montgomery, Alabama. Their stories about that historic march were mesmerizing and made the journey to Forsyth County fly by. Their presence also fortified my strength and helped me set aside my fears. Secretly, I hoped the bus ride would not end; I was surrounded by loving, courageous, interesting, caring Black people and it was one of the most affirming and heartwarming times in my life.

The safety of the bus ride did end, however, and rather abruptly.

When we arrived at our destination in late afternoon, a federal marshal carrying a sophisticated military-type gun boarded our bus to warn us that we needed to be back on the bus before sundown to reduce the chances of uncontrollable violence. An NAACP organizer then admonished us to be sure to hold hands and walk in lines of ten to twelve people across. "Never let go of the people on each side of you," he commanded. The outside positions in the lines, those closest to the angry Forsyth County residents, were intentionally filled by the strongest men. Everything pointed to potential violence.

I remember seeing Klan members in full regalia at the protest. They were frighteningly full of racial hatred, as were all the citizens of the county who had come out to protest the protesters. Federal marshals, FBI agents, and Georgia Bureau of Investigation agents—hundreds of them—formed two long lines to keep the estimated 25,000 marchers separate and safe from the residents. Our protest march was limited to walking down the corridor the agents had defined for us. As I recalled how the residents yelled, screamed, and spit on some of us, it occurred to me that this historic event took place only two years before my daughter was born. This wasn't history yet; the Klan was now and now my Black daughter wanted to know more about them.

As I snapped out of my reverie, I took a long, deep breath and refocused my attention on my daughter. I affirmed her knowledge that the KKK used to kill Black people but that we had better laws now that punished them severely if they tried to do that today. She understands that I am a lawyer and takes great pride in this, so I tried to appeal to her belief in "law." She thinks laws are always effective and something everyone obeys because they are laws. For the longest time, I could not park anywhere or make any kind of traffic move without her asking if what I was doing was "illegal." It drove me nuts. By invoking the law as a shield that would protect her from the KKK, then, I played into her belief in obeying the law.

"Why did they kill Black people? Do Black people kill White people?" she asked.

I said, "Yes, people of different colors do kill each other, but it isn't right and they get punished when they do that."

"They go to jail, right, Mama?"

I said, "That's right." And then I chuckled because it reminded me of her punishment for bad guys, which she explained to me years before. She would punish the bad guys by sending them to jail without pillows. "That will teach them to be good," she concluded. I reminded her of this and we both laughed and thoughts about the KKK drifted off as we turned to Dr. Seuss.

SOMETIMES THE CHALLENGES RACISM POSES OVERWHELM ME

The next day, I called my best friend (a White woman who helped raise two Black foster children) and told her about this KKK talk I had with my daughter. I asked my friend how she would have handled it. We agreed that I had to acknowledge the existence of the KKK and the presence of racial hatred in our society.

"All you can do is answer her questions and talk about things until she is comfortable," my friend reassured me.

"But it doesn't seem fair," I bemoaned. "She's only six years old and she has to know about such ugly things in this world because they touch her so personally."

"It isn't fair," said my friend, "but that's the way it is until things change, which won't be for a long time, I'm afraid."

"You know what is so frustrating?" I asked my friend. "It is frustrating because I always thought I would be able to explain these kinds of things to her in time, in ways she could understand as she got older. Now I know they are sneaking up on her in her own little world outside of our world together. I can't be there to protect her from the racism," I explained. "And you know what else? It's beginning to hit me that I can never adequately explain this to her and I don't think she'll ever understand it because all this racism makes no sense. It's irrational! So no matter how old she is, she'll always be wondering, 'Why?' "

"She's going to be fine," my friend comforted me. "Yes, she will always struggle with racism, and she'll do her part to try to end it. I'll bring some books over for you to read and maybe they'll help, but there aren't any easy answers to this, as I'm sure you know."

I hung up the phone and wondered how people of color struggle with daily bombardments of fear and frustration. I wondered if parents of color know how to cope better with racism, perhaps, because of their lifelong struggles with racism. On the other hand, perhaps watching their children cope with racism is especially difficult precisely because they *know* how much their children hurt because they hurt, too. I was reminded of Du Bois's lament on the death of his infant son. He wrote:

> Well sped, my boy, before the world had dubbed your ambition inso-
> lence, had held your ideals unattainable, and taught you to cringe and
> bow. Better far this nameless void that stops my life than a sea of sor-
> row for you.[33]

Du Bois's comments reflect the enormous sorrow of a father losing his son, who also realized as a father that he would face inevitable and im-measurable pain at knowing his son would be brutally mistreated by White society if the son had lived. I cannot think of a more dramatic statement about the pain of racism because it is difficult for a loving parent to imagine life without his or her child. Usually, a parent resigns himself or herself to this pain only when death would alleviate the child's inevitable and unbearable suffering—typically caused by a fatal illness. White parents have little, if any, understanding that escaping the pain of racism can be seen as "the brighter side" of a Black child's death.

My fears about my daughter's physical safety also reflect other con-cerns. Will she be the victim of hate crimes? Will she encounter Ku Klux Klan members, perhaps without even knowing it? Will her teacher be a Klan member? Will he or she be supportive of White supremacy? Her boss? As any Black person knows all too well, the possibilities for being victimized because of one's Blackness are exponential.

In addition to the fear for her physical safety, I am also worried about her emotional safety. My worries extend beyond the school envi-ronment, the parks, and the playgrounds. Like a shadow, racism follows us everywhere we go. Even in our most vulnerable moments, there it is, adding an extra layer to our vulnerability. Here I relate two stories.

The Hospital

Recently, my daughter was admitted to the university hospital by ambulance because she complained of severe abdominal pain in the middle of the night and I thought her appendix had burst. I rode to the hospital in the cab of the ambulance driven by a White male paramedic. I could hear my daughter screaming and writhing in pain. My attention was totally focused on her and I only half-engaged in the conversation started by the driver, until it turned ugly:

Driver: "Do you know your daughter has tattoos on her stomach?"
Me: "Yes."
Driver: "Do you know where she got them?"
Me: "Sure. She got them at the bowling alley." I thought this was an odd conversation and deduced that he was trying to divert my attention from my daughter in an effort to calm me down.
Driver: "Do you know that's how LSD is transmitted these days? You know. The tattoos are laced with LSD, the kids get them on their skin, and the drug is absorbed by their bodies. If the tattoos are on their stomachs, it can cause severe abdominal pain."

This snapped me out of my daze because it occurred to me that the driver was diagnosing my daughter's illness.

Me: "Oh, my god. You think her tattoos are real, don't you? Well, they aren't! They are the kind you stick on with water and wash off with water. Everyone at the slumber party last night put some on. It's a fun thing. Totally harmless. My daughter is not a drug addict!"

Total silence, except for the siren. The driver and I had no more to say to each other. I wiped the tears away from my eyes and tried not to let him hear me cry. I was unsuccessful, but he said nothing to comfort me. I was glad he didn't try. For just one minute I wanted to be able to concentrate on my daughter in a semipublic place without having to think about race.

As my daughter was being examined in the emergency room, I was presented with all the admissions forms. Not immediately, though. The initial question to me was, "And will the little girl's mother be here soon?" "I am the mother," I responded. "You mean, you aren't the foster mother?" the attendant asked. "No, I'm the MOTHER mother," I responded, my learned emphatic way of cutting off all conversation about race because I didn't want to deal with the usual stream of negative comments or backhanded compliments. I also had to explain my *true* status to the nurse on the floor after my daughter was admitted.

After several diagnostic tests, it was clear my daughter didn't have appendicitis, but it wasn't clear what she did have. Specialist after specialist came in to interview her and elicit information. One doctor asked me how she was doing in school.

"Her grades are terrific. She's in the gifted class, too." I'm not sure why I threw in that last comment, but I'm glad I did, given the doctor's response.

"Really? The gifted class?" he said only half believing me, as he tilted his head and kept scribbling in his notebook.

"Really!" I removed the question mark from the conversation, nodding my head up and down. "Really!" I repeated for good measure because he hadn't looked up. I could tell he felt more regard for my daughter, based on this information alone, because he immediately warmed up to us. "This is pathetic," I thought and I had mixed feelings about using the "gifted child" card to get the doctors to pay closer attention to her. Under the circumstances, her health mattered more than trying to beat back racial stereotypes. "Why am I always being forced to choose between the practical and the principled?" I wondered. It's an awful feeling. But over the years, I have learned how to do it and have even rationalized it: I do it for my daughter because racism is too tough to conquer and sometimes we need a break; we need things to go our way at least some of the time.

The Dining Table

The racism also has invaded our home. One Saturday while my parents and sisters were visiting us from out of town, an old army buddy of my father's came for brunch. He and his wife had moved to a city close to my home and it was an ideal opportunity for my father and his friend to get together. My sister, the good hostess, tried to engage the man and his wife in conversation by asking them how they liked living in their new hometown. The man answered, "It was great till all those n_____s moved in."

My sisters heard it, too, but my parents are very hard of hearing and missed it. I had two choices. I could let him know I was offended by his language, which is my preference under normal circumstances. After nine years of mediating the color line, I have become much more confident and willing to confront racism. But I would have had to shout the word over and over again before my parents could understand what all the fuss was about. That was beyond me. Instead, I quietly took my plate, excused myself, and went to the kitchen to eat with my daughter and my nieces and nephews. Interestingly, the children never asked me why I joined them; they just included me in their conversations and we had a great time. My sisters came to the kitchen in protest as well, but we decided it would be better for them to stay at the main table with my parents, who didn't have a clue what was going on.

My sisters related later that day that the man's wife apologized for her husband's comment. I also received a written apology from him later that week. The apologies are clear evidence that even though the man and his wife were aware that the word is offensive, it is so central to their way of thinking about Blacks that it was a part of their everyday language. Without a second thought, they used it as guests in the house of a Black child!

From a more positive perspective, the apologies also offer hope that even White people who are indoctrinated in the precept of White superiority and Black inferiority, as the man and his wife were, are able to recognize and acknowledge the harm their attitudes cause. Upon receiving the man's apology, I decided to write him back and accept it. I also surprised myself because I was able to tell him that he and his wife should plan to return to my home the next time my parents were in town. I assured him that I had not mentioned the incident to my parents, because I know that if I had, that would have created a rift between them. I didn't want to hurt my parents, but I also have learned that more progress toward racial equality can be achieved if Whites who are actively working to end racism keep open their lines of communication with Whites who are not.

To be assaulted with racist epithets in one's own home is stark evidence that there are few safe places for Blacks to escape racism. Most important, the dining table incident made me realize something that all persons of color know too well from their own experiences: a parent cannot protect his or her child from racism. Nor can parents, alone, undo the harm racism inflicts on our children. When our children are kept out of programs that would be beneficial to them, when they are treated unfairly because of their skin color, when they are negatively stereotyped, when their self-esteem is undermined on a daily basis, it is difficult for the individual family to overcome the overwhelming, generalized assaults on the child of color. Sometimes the assaults are not directed at our own child, but because our children are members of racial minority groups, we *see* how people of color are mistreated throughout society. We also see how much more favorably White people are treated. As children observe the world around them, each and every child, regardless of race, is evaluating where they fit into the power scheme.

Some days, my thoughts wander back to the adoption process. Before I was even asked about race, sex, health, age, background, or anything about what I wanted or could handle in a child, the agency *presumed* I wanted a White child. The first thing I was told by agency officials was that "Any White child we would consider placing with you will have to be HIV positive." The agency's bias about same-race placements took priority over everything else, including my input and my ability to handle falling in love with a child only to have her die from HIV infection within a few years, which was what the medical prognosis was at the time. I told the agency I could not handle that kind of heartbreak and the health of the baby was the single most important factor for me. I could handle certain physical and mental limitations, but I did not want to become attached to a child who was likely to die.

Another point about the adoption process bears mentioning. I also told the adoption personnel that I preferred a girl over a boy. I grew up with three sisters and no brothers. I felt that raising a boy would be "too foreign" to me and I didn't think I could do as good a job. I now realize how unconscious my own racism was at the time. I was aware of my limitations with respect to differences between the sexes. With respect to racial differences, however, not only was I not aware that huge obstacles lay ahead for me raising a Black child, but I also was unrealistically overly confident to believe that I could mediate my way through difficult racial incidents involving my daughter. Clearly, if I thought raising a boy would have been too big a challenge for me, I should have known that raising a Black child would have presented unique challenges as well. Instead, I assumed gender differences were significant and racial differences were not. I was wrong. But this does not mean that transracial adoptions should not be allowed, as I talk about in more detail in chapter 7; however, I want to address some concerns now.

Ironically, the only reason my daughter was placed with me, a single mother, is because she is biracial; race drove the placement decision. Biracial children are considered "special needs" children in the state where I adopted my daughter because they are considered neither White nor Black. As a single mother, I was considered a less than ideal adoptive parent. From the state's perspective, we were a perfect match because the policy operated on the premise that neither a White couple nor a Black couple would want a biracial daughter, and I should consider myself lucky to be able to adopt at all as a single woman.

The talk with my daughter about the KKK left me wondering about the current controversy surrounding the question of whether Black children should be eligible for adoption only by Black parents even though White parents wish to adopt them. A policy requiring Black children to remain in foster care awaiting suitable Black adoptive parents is premised on the notion that a Black child will have a greater understanding of his or her racial identity if he or she is raised by Black parents. This undoubtedly is true, as I explore in more detail in chapter 7. Parents and children go through a long honeymoon period in which the child adores the parent and wants to be like the parent in every conceivable way. This kind of adoration surprised me and made me uncomfortable as I began to realize what was happening with my daughter. She has even remarked that she wants to be White like me, although, fortunately, I have not heard her say this since she was about seven. Admittedly, having a Black parent or Black parents might be better for her because it is difficult for her to cope with the pervasive racism in our society and Black parents know better than White parents what it means to be a child of color in a predominantly White world. Moreover, Black parents can affirm and provide security about a Black child's racial identity in ways a White parent cannot.

Significantly, however, in my daughter's situation, like that of other children of color, the critical question often becomes whether having a parent of a different color is better than having no parent at all. Ironically, my daughter's foster parents were White and they also had another Black child placed with them at the time my daughter lived there. The other child, a boy, was nine months older than my daughter and he was still in foster care on my daughter's first birthday. After that year, we lost touch with the foster family and I do not know what happened to the child.

I have to believe my daughter is better off with a permanent placement with a White mother who tries to instill in her a positive self-image, including being a Black girl, than she would be in the foster care system where she probably would not know a stable family life at all. However, my experiences convince me that transracial adoptions should be last resorts. Until society makes it easier for Blacks to adopt, the foster care problem for Black children will persist and transracial adoptions will offer a better alternative.

Thus, White parents have a special duty to cross the color line into their children's world rather than make their children assimilate into White society. When my daughter says she wants to be just like me, including being White, my response to her is critical in helping her develop a positive racial identity. Like every parent, I have to help my child create a positive self-image. For my daughter, this includes helping her be proud to be Black in a predominantly White world—a world in which I am White and different from her. So I do everything I can to help her develop the positive self-image every child needs. This includes pointing out other differences between us. Some of our differences reflect characteristics we cannot choose: she has naturally curly hair and I have naturally straight hair (although I perm it); she has no freckles and I had lots when I was her age. Other differences reflect choices we make based on our personalities: she likes to climb trees and catch frogs and I do not; she plays basketball, writes music, draws, dances, and sings, and I have none of these talents. All the differences between us help us be individuals and that is what we love about each other.

Moreover, my daughter gains confidence about her racial identity by visiting our Black friends and interacting with them. She has more confidence when she learns about Black history and sees successful Black leaders. My friend is right; my daughter will learn to cope with the racism and so will I. This doesn't mean it isn't hurtful or that accepting racism is easy. It isn't. It is a challenge and the struggle is unrelenting. As the years go by, however, my daughter and I rely more and more on our spirituality to transcend the racism, which we talk about in chapter 8.

5

DOUBLE TROUBLE
Girls of Color

ON LION KINGS, BARBIE DOLLS, AND BARBER SHOPS

My daughter and I went to see the movie *The Lion King* when she was four years old.[34] For the reader unfamiliar with the movie, it is about a lion's jealousy of his brother who is the Lion King. Next in ascension to be king of the jungle is the Lion King's son. The brother's jealousy causes him to murder the Lion King, making his death look like an accident caused by the Lion King's son. The son is convinced he is responsible for his father's death and is unable to cope with the guilt and sorrow. Accordingly, he flees into the jungle, (temporarily) forsaking his right to be Lion King. Without a King, the animal kingdom deteriorates into chaos while evil forces slowly drain the jungle of life.

Sounds like a harmless journey through the "circle of life," as the theme song would have us believe. Except that race and sex stereotyping permeate the movie. For example, both the Lion King and his son are the typical honey-color of lions, and the jealous brother lion is a dark-complected grayish-black. Before the movie, who had ever seen a black lion? Of the zillions of children's books my daughter and I have read, I don't ever recall seeing a black lion. A purple dinosaur, yes. A cat in a hat, yes. A bear cooking in the kitchen, yes. We've even seen a flying elephant. Some pretty imaginative animal scenes have come our way, but never a black lion, especially one that comes from a family of blondes. Curiously, of all the imaginative animal characters that Disney has created, it was strange that Disney colored the lifelike lions not fantasy hues, but rather hues that portrayed human skin pigmentation. If

Disney artists did not intentionally color the lions to invoke the stereotypes "good guys are light" (white) and "bad guys are dark" (black),
they nevertheless perpetuated these stereotypes.

Moreover, Disney artists' (unconscious) racism was evident in other
characters in the movie. For example, at the bottom of the animal peck-
ing order were the laughing hyenas, also dark-complected, which are
portrayed as the most evil and untrustworthy animals in the kingdom.
But Disney outdid itself with the hyenas by characterizing them as a "racial other" through cultural stereotypes. I thought Disney wanted viewers to see the hyenas as Blacks who spoke broken English, ate barbecued
chicken, and lazed around all day. A few of my Latino friends walked
away from the movie thinking Disney had invoked the worst stereotypes
of Latino culture to portray the hyenas. Clearly, viewers who are sensitive to racial differences agreed that the hyenas were intended to be eth-
nically different in a derogatory way from White middle-class Americans.

Adding the romantic element to the movie, the Lion King's son
loved a blond, female lion who was indecisive and powerless compared
to the future Lion King. For example, rather than assume the leadership
role in the jungle—become the Lion Queen—while the son recovered
from his father's death, she spent her time and energy looking for him
to encourage him to return home and assume his responsibilities. Meanwhile, everything in the jungle is dying. The continuing vitality of the
entire animal kingdom turns on whether she is successful in getting the
son to grow up and act like a man (King). Ultimately, she succeeds, the
son becomes King, she becomes his wife, and jungle life returns to its
vibrant state. All the dead grass and trees become green; all the dried-up
rivers and streams start flowing with fresh, clear blue water; and most
important, the Lion King and his wife stand atop the mountain, ruling
over all the other animals, including the hyenas who continue to live
down in the barren, brown, dark caves but nevertheless are laughingly
happy to be so poverty-stricken.

My description of the movie reveals what I thought about it. In
contrast, my daughter loved the movie and begged me for weeks and
weeks to take her to see it again. I refused, however, because her overwhelmingly positive reaction to the movie did not reflect the negative
feelings it brought out in her. Specifically, my daughter walked out of

the movie and said she wished she were a boy so she could be the Lion King. I chuckled to myself as I realized that in her four-year-old perspective of the world, she had completely missed what is quite obvious to adults. I squeezed her hand and said, "Sweetheart, to be the Lion King, you would have to be a *lion*," and I emphasized that word.

But her comment also confirmed what I had feared: that the movie gave her a message of the inferiority of girls. Thus, my adult response to my daughter's comment was intended to help her put the sexism in perspective. The *real* barrier to her becoming the Lion King was not that she was a girl, but that she was not a lion. Temporarily, I wanted to protect her from the sexism; cover it up with a bigger problem beyond everyone's control so she would not feel it was bad to be a girl, and a Black girl at that. By four years of age, my daughter understood that boys and Whites are privileged; she wanted to be privileged and valued, too, even if it meant giving up her identity as a young Black girl. I couldn't believe it was happening so early in her life. Once she understood that she would have to be a lion to be the Lion King, we talked about why girl lions should also be allowed to be queens just like boy lions can be kings.

Significantly, she did not mention anything about the lions' colors and I felt it better not to go into that aspect of the movie. Focusing on one issue at a time is sufficiently challenging on occasion. Based on her comments about race, however, I am sure the racial implications in the movie did not escape her. If nothing else, Disney subtly indoctrinated its viewers in the precept of White superiority and Black inferiority in the *Lion King*. With a bit of reflection, readers will know that *The Lion King* is not unique on this count; most Disney movies depict race and sex stereotypes.

I decided to use *The Lion King* as a discussion point in one of my seminars on equality at the law school. The seminar was comprised of a racially diverse group of men and women. Surprisingly, most of the students had seen the movie and explained it to the few who had not. Some of the students added their own impressions of the movie's depiction of racial inequality. Two foreign students from Korea and China related how the movie had been banned in their countries because it was a "story of White imperialism." I thought this was a rather severe indictment of the movie: a comment worth reflection. It was also the first time the women had ever said anything in the seminar and I wanted the American students to respect the foreign students' courage to voice their opinions. Instead, the foreign students' comments were ignored and the conversation was dominated by two White men and one White woman.

The three students vociferously reacted in disbelief to the criticism of the movie. For example, one of them quickly pointed out that the movie could not have been racist because James Earl Jones and Whoopi Goldberg were the voice-overs for the Lion King and one of the hyenas, respectively. Because Jones and Goldberg are Black, the students concluded that they would not have participated in making the movie if they thought it perpetuated racism against Blacks. Disney's inclusion of a Black actor and actress conclusively proved to them that the movie was not racist. Interestingly, even some Black students seemed persuaded by this argument.

Building on the momentum, one White man joined in, expressing *hostility* to the suggestion that the movie reinforced the messages of White/male superiority and Black/female inferiority. His voice and demeanor reflected his anger at the *mere suggestions* that the movie promoted the subordination of Blacks and women. He indignantly exclaimed, "Well, if you want us to believe *The Lion King* is racist, I suppose next week you'll be telling us *Beauty and the Beast* is sexist." I think this comment was supposed to be the final word—the ultimate proof that some of us were crazy to think what we did about the movie. Instead, most of the women laughed (I bit my lip trying not to join them), because his comment was the best proof of our point: What Disney movie isn't sexist, we wondered? The laughter was met with the vociferous White woman's comment that some of us were simply "reading too much into a children's story."

The Lion King sends some positive messages, as one of my friends relates. It takes place in Africa, exposing children to positive aspects of African culture. It also presents a picture of the interconnectedness of different kinds of animals who strive to achieve harmony living together.

Positive messages can be conveyed to children without also conveying to them negative messages suggesting Blacks, Latinos, and women are inferior to Whites and men. *The Lion King*'s theme that peace and harmony can only be achieved if the white, male lion is king is presented as a "natural" order—as the way things are supposed to be. From a child's perspective the distinctions between reality and fantasy are not always clear, and it takes little imagination for a child to extrapolate from this message and apply it to people. Fiction and fantasy are primary ways for children to learn about life and social relationships. My daughter's wish to be a boy after seeing *The Lion King* reflects "normal" child development. Similarly, my friend's son who is Black wanted to be king after he saw the movie and wondered if it was possible for there to be a Black king. Quite telling.

Whether *The Lion King*'s positive messages outweigh the negative race and sex stereotypes in the film is a question each parent has to decide. To me, as an educator and a mother, my daughter's and the students' reactions to the movie were disturbing. As an educator, I was disappointed in my seminar students. Rather than engaging in an intellectual discussion about the media's role in the depiction of racial minorities and women as inferior to Whites and men, the vociferous students employed unsophisticated debating tactics to silence their classmates who disagreed with them and summarily dismissed as implausible and unworthy of serious consideration the notion that Disney could make a racist and sexist movie.

Yet the movie poignantly demonstrates the pervasiveness of unconscious racism. Employing James Earl Jones and Whoopi Goldberg as voice-overs in the film illustrates that an individual's race alone does not make him or her "above being racist" or incapable of perpetuating racism. Unconscious racism exists even in goodwill people—Black and White—because the subtlety of the message escapes even the messenger. Once this is pointed out, however, it is the response that is critical. Denying the racism in *The Lion King* allows it to go unchallenged, increasing the probability that Disney will employ similar tactics in future films.

As a closely related issue, to me as a mother, the seminar discussion was disappointing because it reinforced my frustration at trying to combat negative stereotyping of Blacks and women. Unfortunately, the messages of inferiority are learned by Black children and little girls beginning at birth. Disney's presence in most American households seems inevitable and its influence on children cannot be overstated. If graduate students taking a course on race and sex equality are unable to entertain serious thoughts about these kinds of issues, I wonder as a mother whether there is hope for persuading institutions like Disney that they are promoting the inequality of Black children and girls in their films.

My frustration grew when one of the most outspoken White men in the class came to my office the following day to meet with me privately. He informed me that he had rented the movie and watched it several times the preceding evening. He handed me his list of reasons why the movie was not racist or sexist. He quickly added that he did not want me to share his list with the class; it was intended only for my "edification"—his word choice.

I wondered why the student, a graduating senior, would bother to rent the movie, study it, and put so much effort into convincing me that I was wrong about the *Lion King*? If only students in my other classes put as much effort into their work outside the class, I thought. His reaction to the class discussion seemed like an overreaction. But I could not imagine why it was important to him for me to change my mind about the *Lion King*. And if he was so troubled by the class discussion, why didn't he share his thoughts with the whole class and try to persuade his classmates that they were wrong, too? I concluded that he met with me privately because, on some level, he knew there was merit to our critical analysis of the *Lion King* and he felt outnumbered in the classroom setting but desperately wanted us to be wrong. In my experience, it is difficult for Whites and men, generally, to confront racism and sexism.

As the mother of a Black girl, I want to protect my daughter from the harm stereotypes do to her self-esteem as a *girl* and as a *Black*. Combating one kind of stereotype at a time is sufficiently difficult, but when race and sex stereotypes are combined as they arguably are in the *Lion King*, it is especially hard to overcome them. To my surprise and chagrin, however, the double trouble of stereotypes arises far more often than I had realized prior to becoming the mother of a Black girl.

For example, on my daughter's Christmas list a few years ago was one startling request: she wanted a "My Size Barbie." As the name implies, "My Size Barbie" stands three feet tall and is larger than life if you are only six years old. Barbie also is attached to a roll-along platform, making it easy for a child to take her by the hand and pull her along wherever the child goes. When my daughter played with Barbie, I usually knew where she was in the house because I could hear them rolling back and forth across our wooden floors. Getting around outside was trickier, but my daughter's solution to that problem was to stand Barbie up in her red wagon and pull her up and down the street, across the yard, or wherever they needed to go. Perched in the wagon, Barbie towered over my daughter and it looked like my daughter was pulling a miniature float in a one-person parade. I'm sure our neighbors got a few good laughs, as did I, watching my daughter and Barbie walking up and down the street, undoubtedly engaged in delightful conversations.

When I read my daughter's Christmas list and saw that she wanted a Barbie doll, I had mixed feelings. I had always promised myself that if I ever had a daughter, I wouldn't buy her a Barbie doll because of the negative stereotypes about girls and women that Barbie personifies. Her model-like looks alone are enough to offend most mothers. Or, as my friend once commented, "How many women do you know with aerodynamic bodies?" On the other hand, my daughter's request may have meant she wanted to explore the "girlish" side of her personality—the side that seemed to have been put on hold. I decided Barbie posed little threat on that score.

In another significant way, however, Barbie was somewhat threatening. I was disappointed that my daughter's first request for a doll was Barbie because Barbie also fits a racial stereotype of the preferred woman in our society—the white, blonde, blue-eyed woman. My daughter does not have any of these features. (And the *only* thing Barbie and I have in common is our skin color, which rules out my daughter's desire to get Barbie because Barbie looks like me.) When I talked about my reservations with a friend, my friend told me that I could get my daughter a Black Barbie. I thought she was kidding, but it was true.

I told my daughter that maybe Santa would bring her a Barbie who was brown, just like her. I was smiling with this news and very hopeful that my daughter would understand the significance of what I was saying. *("I can get you Barbie and justify my decision because she is Black.")* Instead, she looked horrified and immediately rejected the idea. "I want the White Barbie, not the Black one. If Santa can't bring the White one, then maybe he can bring something else," she said, rather forcefully. I tried to get her to talk about her preference for the White Barbie, but she offered no explanation. "Just because," was all she would say.

"Oh, great," I thought. It's just like the Power Rangers, except that with Barbie my daughter was evidencing some pride in being a girl. For whatever reasons, though, my daughter was not ready to play with a Black "My Size Barbie."

My worries that Barbie would teach my daughter to value negative stereotypes about girls were unfounded—at least so far. If anything, given the tomboy in her, it is remarkable that she will have anything to do with any doll. One of the biggest issues we dealt with about gender stereotypes centered around haircuts.

At one point, my daughter wanted to be bald. It started when she was four years old and went to a barber shop with one of her four-year-old boyfriends and his mother. After her friend was finished getting his crew cut, my daughter climbed into the barber's chair and asked for the "same thing." This news came to me when my friend called me at work to ask what she should have done. For a brief moment, I didn't know what my friend had told the barber and I wondered if my daughter's beautiful, soft, black curls had been chopped off. The thought upset me considerably. I remember thinking that I hoped my friend didn't give the barber permission to cut my daughter's hair, but I also was relieved that I wasn't there to make the decision. What would be my reason for not giving her permission to have a crew cut? That I love her black curls shouldn't mean she can't cut them off if she wants to. "So, what happened?" I asked my friend. "What does her hair look like?"

"Don't worry," my friend said, "the barber wouldn't cut her hair at all. This really upset her, too. She refused to get out of the chair and told the barber he wasn't treating her equally. The barber looked at me and I told him it was okay to cut it. I hope that's what you would have said. I didn't know what to say. It'll grow back. But the barber said he wasn't used to cutting little girls' hair and he would rather we go next door to the beauty salon. So we left."

"So did you go to the beauty parlor?" I asked.

"No. No. She was too upset with not being treated equally with the boys and refused to go to a 'girls' barber,' as she called it."

I was relieved, but the incident left me unsettled. My daughter had it right, on the one hand. Why shouldn't she be able to ask the barber to cut her hair in a crew cut? So long as the guardian of the child (my friend) said it was okay, why should he care? Ironically, I was getting irritated, even though I was relieved my daughter still had her curls. I was also proud of her for standing up for her sense of justice and her need to be treated equally.

I thought about what had happened. It is socially acceptable for boys to get crew cuts, but it is not socially acceptable for girls to get crew cuts. As a mother of a little girl, even I was somewhat uncomfortable with her getting a crew cut. I thought about the significance of the crew cut to military discipline and how it is used to instill a strong, aggressive sense of masculinity in military personnel. When Shannon Faulkner was admitted to the Citadel as the first woman cadet in the school's history, she, like every new cadet, had her head shaved. The story was reported as if shaving the heads of the cadets is a particularly heinous act, especially when it is a woman's head that gets shaved. Many news accounts reported this story before Ms. Faulkner actually enrolled in the college, suggesting she might forgo attending the Citadel because of the requirement that she cut her hair. The symbolic significance of baldness to masculinity and its antithesis, the defeminization that baldness does to women, was perceived by many people as a sufficient reason for Ms. Faulkner to drop her ambitions of becoming the first woman graduate of the school. Thus, when the barber refused to cut my daughter's hair in a crew cut, he was imposing a gender role stereotype on my daughter—a stereotype with remarkable significance in a male-dominated world.

I reflected further. There is another dimension to the crew cut story, a dimension that relates to being an African American woman. It is quite common for African American women to wear their hair in very short styles, including the equivalent of crew cuts. In the African American community, women with extremely short-cropped hair are seen as beautiful; the distinctive hairstyle is a symbol of African American unity. Thus, the barber's refusal to cut my daughter's hair promoted a gender stereotype, but a gender stereotype that is not true for African American women. If the barber had been able to bring himself to break down his assumptions about how a little (White) girl should look by giving my daughter the crew cut, his decision also would have reflected his acknowledgment about a cultural difference between White and African American women. Unfortunately, the barber's belief in traditional gender stereotypes, coupled with his apparent lack of knowledge about racial differences between White and Black women, resulted in a decision that nullified my daughter's independent judgment about how she wanted to appear as a young, African American girl.

As I was bathing my daughter after her trip to the barber, she told me how unequally the barber had treated her. I tried to defend the barber, suggesting he had his own views about what little girls should look like. Again, she said boys and girls should be treated equally. I agreed with her, but knew this issue with the hair was not over and that sooner or later I was going to be faced with backing up her decision to have her hair cut off. I knew my hairdresser would do it if I asked, but I secretly hoped we might make it through the tomboy stage with most of her hair. But that wasn't to be.

The time finally came when she was six and in first grade. She asked if she could have her head shaved. In the two years since we escaped the crew cut with the barber, she had decided she wanted an even more drastic look—baldness. I have to admit that I was opposed to this, but I didn't know how to voice my concerns. Part of my problem was, I didn't know what my concerns were. What was I worried about? Was I worried people would think she is a boy? But so what? I thought. I think it would be good to break down the stereotypes. Her classmates and everyone around us know she is a girl, so that shouldn't bother me. But who cares even if strangers think she is a boy? What difference does it make? Okay, so that wasn't a good reason to object. Moreover, I knew that many African American women wear very, very short haircuts. This could be her statement of racial identity, a statement that escaped the barber and came to me only on reflection.

"I'm not sure this is a good idea, sweetheart," I told her.

"But why, Mom? It's my hair. Why can't I cut it off?"

Searching for some kind of answer, I mumbled something like, "But your friends might make fun of you and it takes a while for it to grow back. What if it makes you uncomfortable?" I really was concerned about other kids making fun of her, but even as I said this, I realized how silly this response was. Imagine if the situation had been reversed and I was trying to get her to cut her hair a particular way and she resisted me because other kids might make fun of her. What would I say? What any parent would say. I would say she needs to make up her own mind and not do things according to what other people will think. That's what I would say.

"Mom," she said emphatically, "nobody makes fun of Michael Jordan!" This time I had missed the obvious. So part of it was about racial identity. She wanted to be like Michael Jordan. I had to agree with her that no one makes fun of him, and I did not point out to her that no one would dare make fun of him because he is seven feet tall. In her six-year-old view of the world, she was just like him—Black. So shaving her head was a matter of identifying with a Black hero. I had to let her do it.

"And besides, Mom, I can always wear a hat if I don't like it."

That settled it. My daughter was going to go through a bald stage. And, sure enough, we did.

I did use the haircut theme, however, to discuss with my daughter the concept of equality between boys and girls. I thought perhaps I wasn't making it very clear that girls can do anything that boys can do. If my daughter understood this, she might take greater pride in being a girl. I wanted her to be proud to be a girl and openly defy the stereotypes.

The time came for discussing this when she was scheduled for her first-grade school picture. I suggested she might want to wear a dress for the picture, but I wasn't hopeful. She hadn't had a school picture in a dress since she was three. She hadn't had on a dress since she was three, except for the occasional fairy princess dress-up dress, but that was strictly make-believe, "You know the difference, right, Mom?" "Yes, dear," I would always say. I thought I would tackle the issue head on.

"You know, sweetheart, boys and girls can do everything the same. Anything a boy can do, you can do, too. It doesn't matter whether you wear a dress, or whether you have long hair or short hair, or anything. Boys and girls are equal." I tried to appeal to her sense of equality.

"Oh, no, Mom. You are wrong. Girls can't do everything boys can do."

"Oh? They can't? Well, tell me, what is it you want to do that you can't do as a girl?" I asked, truly curious. I thought I had her on this one, but I was wrong, much to my surprise.

"I want to be the Pope, Mom. You have to be a boy to be the Pope. See, I told you boys and girls aren't equal."

I did laugh. I couldn't help it, although I didn't want her to think I was laughing at her. But her response was so clever. That must be the only answer she could have given me to prove my theory wrong.

As I was laughing, I pulled her to me and said, "Sweetheart, you know what? We aren't even Catholic and the Pope has to be Catholic." I didn't even touch the issue of race or mention how slim the odds were for a Black person to become Pope. No, I'd stick to the Catholic issue like I stuck with the lion issue earlier.

She didn't know what I was talking about and looked bewildered. I imagined this conversation, as if I were talking to a much older child.

"There's a bigger hurdle, you mean, to becoming Pope other than being a girl?" she would ask. "Now you're telling me you have to be Catholic, too?"

"That's right, but you can convert and become Catholic. But I don't know if the Pope's ever been a converted Catholic. Maybe you have to be born Catholic to be Pope. Not that I want to discourage you, though . . ."

When I told one of my friends this story, she laughed, too, and then suggested I should have told my daughter how great it would be for her to be Pope because the Pope wears dresses. Why didn't I think of that?

From her first crew cut at the age of six, my daughter has had several more. She alternates between crew cuts and long hair, with maybe a month of her-hair-looks-really-nice moments in between the extremes. Undoubtedly, the shorter her hair, the more times she is called a boy by strangers. When she was in the tomboy stage, she thought this was great.

Gradually, though, she grew out of that stage. In third grade, she actually wore a dress to school—once, maybe twice. And the crew cuts were becoming rarer and rarer. As she became increasingly more proud to be a girl, she would politely but firmly correct people who called her a boy. I remember once when we were checking out at the grocery store. She had just had her ears pierced, which was supposed to make it crystal clear to anyone that she was a girl. The cashier, however, missed the obvious and called her a boy. My daughter didn't say a word. Rather, she grabbed her pierced ears and waved them in the cashier's face. It worked. The cashier apologized and my daughter smiled her sheepish smile. Progress.

Notwithstanding the progress she was making outside her classroom in letting the world know she is a girl, the issue seemed to persist within the classroom. Surprisingly, the confusion was coming not from her classmates, but from the teacher who insisted on referring to her in the male pronoun. This was understandable the first few days of class before the teacher got to know the children. After that, it became inexcusable. No matter how much my daughter got upset with the teacher for doing this, the teacher persisted. I met with the teacher several times to ask her to stop it and to call my daughter a girl. Even as a tomboy, my daughter never gave up her identity as a girl. The teacher assured me it was a slip of the tongue and that, of course, she knew my daughter was a girl.

My daughter stopped complaining about it and I thought the teacher had finally gotten it! One day, a few weeks before the end of the school year, however, my sister picked up my daughter from school and ran into the teacher. Four times during their short conversation the teacher referred to my daughter as a "he." Each time my sister corrected the teacher, but to no avail. I couldn't believe it was still happening. I asked my daughter why she hadn't said anything to me. She answered, "Oh, Mom. I've gotten used to it. She'll never change."

This was unsatisfactory to me and the next day I confronted the teacher's aide about it. Another parent who frequently visited the class told me that my daughter's gender had become a joke in the class. I asked what she meant. The parent replied, "It's a joke. Ms. [teacher's name] calls Mary a boy. The children laugh and correct her, almost in unison. The teacher says, 'Of course,' and then she does it again and the process repeats itself all day long."

I was angry to think of my daughter enduring this humiliation day after day. When I asked her how it made her feel, she said, "Silly. Like, how can Ms. [teacher's name] not know I'm a girl?" Good question. I wanted an answer, too. But, naturally, the teacher denied that she continued to do it. There were only two more weeks of school and my daughter asked me to forget it. It was embarrassing to talk about it.

The teacher's indifference to my daughter's needs was unprofessional. For a whole school year, she chipped away and undermined my daughter's self-esteem as a girl. Critically important, the teacher's disrespect for my daughter also reflected her disdain for my daughter's Blackness, which was an essential part of my daughter's identity as well. In other words, the teacher's disrespect for my daughter was total; it is impossible to partially disrespect someone. Indeed, perhaps my daughter's race was the *real* reason the teacher didn't like my daughter. It is impossible to believe the teacher's behavior was unconscious or even semiconscious; she simply was confronted too many times on the issue not to be aware that she was hurting my daughter.

To date, this teacher's behavior has been the most blatant example of a *sustained* disdain for Blacks and especially Black girls *and I was unable to stop the teacher from hurting my daughter.* Because my daughter didn't complain about it after my last conference with the teacher, I naively believed the teacher when she said it wouldn't happen again and it certainly never happened in my presence. When I wasn't around the school, the behavior continued and my daughter, perhaps seeing that the teacher hadn't listened to me, simply decided to take the abuse. Who knows how many Black children surrender to unfairness because their parents are unable to successfully mediate the color line or because they have become so accustomed to the mistreatment?

I hope I never resign myself to stop trying to mediate across the color line, although I have learned to choose my fights. I now understand that I cannot take on every racist or sexist unfairness inflicted on my daughter because there are too many even to recount and I don't even know about some of them. If we tried to challenge every display of racial mistreatment, my daughter and I would have no life. We won't let White society have that much influence and control over us. More important, I don't want my daughter to lose her entire childhood to the horror of racial discrimination. Our joyous and loving times are too precious.

6

LIVING WITH RACISM

Responses to the Stories

I started this book years ago when my daughter was only six. At the time, I did not plan to publish it and wrote down the stories more for the purpose of keeping a journal. Two years into the project, I entertained the idea of this book, but I was not enthusiastic about it because I was not sure it was the right thing to do. Like every loving parent, I do not want to hurt my daughter and I asked myself such questions as: If the public knew these stories, would they shun us even more? Would children tease my daughter? Would teachers resent us for being so "sensitive"? Would I become the "race police" in our hometown? The possible backlash in our lives that might happen as a result of publishing this book is a serious consideration. To move forward with it, I had to believe that the book would do more good than harm.

My hesitation was compounded because when I started keeping a journal, my daughter was very young and I could not discuss the matter with her in a meaningful way. Fortunately, one of the blessings that has resulted from my hesitation is her growing maturity. My daughter is now ten years old and we have talked about the project and she has even written something for the book, which appears in chapter 8. The time also has allowed me to process my new awareness of the depth of racism. Initially, I was so taken aback by it that I became depressed and let racism get the better of me. With much reflection and reading, and through writing this book, I have learned the importance of spirituality in the struggle against injustice. My hope is that with this new perspective and optimism, the book is better than it would have been had I followed through on it several years ago.

I share this background because I think it is important for readers to appreciate the complexities in the decision to publish the book. As a mother, I wanted to be clear in my mind and heart about my reasons for writing this book. From what I have learned from loving my daughter, it is important to speak out about racial mistreatment. I want other White people of goodwill to share our stories so that they will be motivated to help end racism. My experiences as a White person of goodwill tell me that other Whites would appreciate these stories because they truly are good-hearted people and do not understand the depth of racism in America. As the following stories reveal, many friends and colleagues encouraged me to follow through with this project.

ON SUNS, MOONS, AND EASTER BUNNIES

My daughter and I were having a mother–daughter talk one evening when she was only seven years old.

"Mom, is it true that when people get too close to the sun their skin gets darker?"

"Yes, sweetheart. That's true." I quickly tried to remember all the lessons I had learned in eighth-grade science so that I could sound somewhat intelligent in trying to explain the science of skin pigmentation.

"Well, if that's true," she said with her head held low, "then I'm going far away from that sun. I'm going to fly to the moon because it's no fun being dark."

I held her close to me, silently screaming: "Oh, please don't go to the moon. You're safe here. You're beautiful. We're working on it, sweetheart. We're working on it."

As I look back on our years together, I am overwhelmed to think of all the hurtful racial incidents my daughter has endured in her short life; the cumulative effect of the harm summed up in her desire to go to the moon to be safe. At the same time, when I tell some of the stories in this book at educational symposia and colloquia around the country, I am encouraged that many Whites are open to hearing them. I want to share some of those responses because they give me strength. Equally important, the responses offer evidence that America is concerned about racial injustice and they also offer tidbits of hope that we can transcend racism.

REMEMBER THE PURSE?

As I tell the story of the woman and her lost purse in the Boston airport, every audience is utterly surprised that my daughter was accused of stealing it. In turn, I am somewhat surprised that the audience is not able to anticipate that this is going to be the "punch line" to the story. I became aware of the audience's surprise when one particular group let out an audible, collective gasp as I repeated the woman's accusation, "I bet that Black kid took it!" The audiences' responses tell me that they, too, are shocked at what they are learning from the stories. Like me and most people who believe in racial equality, they are moved by the injustices related in the stories.

That the audience members are surprised by the stories also evidences and confirms my sense that most Whites are not fully aware of racism and how pervasive it is in our society. Like me at one time a few years ago, what other response could they have had to this story except one of surprise? At one time, it would have been easy and automatic for me to distance myself from the woman in the airport and express spontaneous indignation at her accusation about a Black child. When it happened to my daughter, however, I was almost speechless but certainly personally insulted and immediately became defensive. In other words, I was not a "neutral" liberal White or even a White civil rights lawyer witnessing the unjust accusation; I was a mother witnessing the dehumanization of my daughter based on an unjust stereotype. One's reaction to an incident such as that in the airport necessarily depends on one's perspective. Surprise was the most benign feeling I had, and yet it is most telling of my lack of awareness of racism at the time.

Let me compare White audience members' responses to the stories with those of the Black audience members. Any Black person or person of color predicts the ending to the airport story. I've seen it from the podium. Generally, before I begin my talks, I pan the audience trying to get a feel for who my audience is. One day, as I looked around the room, I realized that most Whites were talking to their neighbors, which I have interpreted as a sign that they were enthusiastically awaiting my comments on race. In contrast, I often see Blacks sitting silently by themselves, which I have interpreted as a sign that they are skeptical that I would have anything meaningful to say about race. I imagine the Blacks saying, "Oh, here's another one of those liberal Whites who's going to talk about race. What does she know?"

And then comes the punch line to the airport story. As Whites gasp in disbelief, one Black audience member yells, "Of course! Of course!" The audiences' demeanor flips at this point; the Blacks sit up and the Whites fall back in their seats. Watching the transition is fascinating and yet also disquieting because it makes me even more aware than I usually am that I am in a never-never land. As the White mother of a Black child, and because I live the day-to-day effects of racism with her as much as a mother can, I am at times neither White nor Black. Naturally, then, both Blacks and Whites question my credibility. Before my talks begin, my skin color aligns me with other liberal Whites. Once I am into the stories, it is clear that I am speaking from across the color line, a place where most Whites never go. Even from across the color line, however, I continue to be White among Black folks who wonder how I got here and what I'm doing. Let me say, it is a journey and I also am trying to figure it out.

I'VE SEEN THE TEARS

Some audience members who hear these stories cry. I gave a keynote address at a conference at my alma mater and my family was able to attend. At the conclusion of the talk, my oldest sister came up to me, hugged me, and with tears in her eyes apologized for perpetuating the myth that color doesn't matter. She confessed that she adhered to the color-blindness philosophy just like many school educators and didn't realize how it can hurt a child of color. As she held me, it occurred to me that this was my daughter's aunt making this confession; my sister loves my daughter very much and now she can love her as a Black niece and my daughter can be a Black niece who loves her White aunt.

Also in this audience with my family was a White woman who has an adopted Black child. Coincidentally, we also are friends and colleagues and she had come to listen to my talk and offer her support. As I told these stories, I kept an eye on her in the audience because I suspected the stories might strike her in a different way from other audience members. I looked for signals from her that told me she understood what I was saying. Early into the talk the affirmation came—she had tears running down her cheeks. And then I could no longer make eye contact with her because I needed all my energy to make it through the talk.

PEOPLE SAY THE STORIES ARE MOVING AND EDUCATIONAL

Many, many people tell me they are moved by the stories and want to know more. A poignant example comes to mind. When I returned home after giving the talk at my alma mater, I received an e-mail message from a first-year law student who had heard my talk. He described himself as a Jewish, White man. He started his message by saying that I didn't know him and that he had not planned to attend my talk. The dean, however, had asked him to videotape the conference proceedings and, consequently, he was a captive audience member. Up to this point in his message, I thought I was supposed to feel sorry that his Saturday had been taken up with the conference and then I read the next few lines and realized why he was writing. He related how moved he had been by the talk and expressed his wish that he could take some classes with me to learn more about what I have learned about racism. In turn, I was quite moved by his message as well; he didn't have to let me know this and yet he had written the e-mail message within an hour of my talk. This means he had to find my e-mail address, because I had not given it to him. I hadn't even left the auditorium at my alma mater and his message was waiting for me a thousand miles away at home.

ON THE LIGHT SIDE

Sometimes a person's response to a particular story can be humorous. A few years ago, at a national conference on gender and race in higher education in Los Angeles,[35] I talked about a self-portrait my daughter has on her bedroom door. It is easily four feet tall and my daughter is wearing a Chicago Bull's basketball uniform with Michael Jordan's number on it. Significantly, there are only three colors in the picture: her uniform is red, her very short-cropped hair is black, and her skin is brown. I mentioned to the audience that without the brown and the black in the picture, my daughter wouldn't look anything like herself.

At the end of my talk, one audience member asked me how my husband and I taught my daughter about racial identity, given that he is Black and I am White. I thought her question interesting and responded that I didn't face that problem because I'm not married. There was some jostling around in the audience as everyone seemed unsettled either with my response or with the woman's assumption that I was married to a Black man.

Quickly, I was taken back in time to the very first days of my daughter's placement with me. Often, when we were out strolling around the neighborhood, someone would stop and comment on what a beautiful baby she was. Inevitably, this was followed with a comment, "I bet her father is very handsome." I didn't take these comments personally; I also was wrapped up in the beauty of my daughter and clearly, at least one of her biological parents was very attractive. Without thinking, I would usually respond that I didn't know the father and added that he had a beautiful smile (which was what I was told by the adoption agency). The person would give me a strange look and eventually I realized what was going on—they thought I was the birth mother. So I quickly added to my comments that I didn't know who the biological mother is, either, and explained that my daughter is adopted. I talk about my daughter so much that I guess I'm beginning to assume that everyone knows she is adopted.

RESPONSES FROM BLACKS ARE TOTALLY DIFFERENT

As a mother, professor, and writer who straddles the color line, I struggle with issues of credibility. I know that my analysis of race in America makes many Whites uncomfortable because it takes most of them closer than they have ever been, perhaps too close, to the color line. Unmasking White racism is a painful process and one that each individual White must go through if America is to end institutional racism.

Thus, when Blacks offer support for my comments, I am especially relieved and encouraged. For example, a Black woman about my age approached me after one of my talks and wanted to share her thoughts about color-blindness. Her experiences with that philosophy were remarkable. Whites would often come up to her and talk about her "prematurely graying hair" or tell her how pretty her dress was, but they would never say anything about her race. She confided in me that their selective sight made her uncomfortable. She deduced that she wasn't supposed to talk about her African American heritage; that her race was supposed to be invisible.

As she told me her stories, the tone in her voice was one of disbelief—disbelief that Whites could really be blind to her Blackness. As a White person who admits that she sees color differences and who denounces the color-blind philosophy, I offered support for her theory that Whites who deny they see color are daft. She offered support for my theory that Blacks want Whites to fess up to the reality that color-blindness is a myth.

This is not to say that I feel completely secure in what I am saying when I give talks or write my articles. Quite the contrary. I am ever mindful that the journey across the color line is a complicated one and one that requires being open to learning about race and also being open to rejecting misconceptions one has about race. Frequently, I am jolted or caught off guard by audience responses. For example, in the middle of telling one of the stories in this book at a faculty luncheon at another school, one of the Black professors walked out. She is a scholar whose work I admire and watching her leave the luncheon upset me considerably. I tried to remain composed, but in the back of my mind I thought I had deeply offended her by something I said.

I finished my comments and as I was chatting with other professors, the colleague who had walked out approached me and asked if I would come back to her office with her. I agreed, fully expecting that she was going to tell me that I had it all wrong or something equally negative along the lines of "What can you know about race as a White person?"

It wouldn't have been the first time I've been challenged, and I thought she was being kind to at least do this in the privacy of her office.

Once inside her office, a few other White women professors joined us. So much for the one-on-one "dress down," I thought. At least the small group was better than the luncheon group. But to my utter surprise, my Black colleague apologized for leaving my talk and said she hoped she hadn't disrupted me. To paraphrase her, she explained that she is "a thick-skinned, middle-aged Black woman who has heard it all and couldn't be hurt by this stuff anymore." She said she had to leave the luncheon because she was "about to burst into tears" hearing some of the stories about my daughter. My eyes started to mist. I was relieved the other women were there to pick up the conversation and give me a moment to compose myself. Those few moments in my Black colleague's office were joyous ones; I had successfully articulated what it feels like to love across the color line.

By far, one of the most difficult responses I have received in telling some of these stories came from a Black mother. She asked me, "What are you doing to protect yourself from all this?" Apparently, I misunderstood her question because I responded that my daughter and I have many Black friends, we do this, we do that. But she interrupted me and said, "No, that's not what I mean. I want to know how you, as a White mother, are coping with the racism. How are you, as the mother of a Black child, protecting yourself from the pain of seeing your child suffer?" Her question left me speechless. In a few seconds, this woman had touched on all my deepest fears and feelings of insecurity. Loving parents put their children first in their lives. My job as the mother is to protect my child and, at times, I feel inadequate to do that. I felt incredibly vulnerable standing before the audience. I was afraid that all the pain inside me was going to burst out in a flood of tears because the truth is, at the time I was asked this question, I knew even less than I know now about how to maneuver through a racist world. And I still am not sure how best to persuade Whites that there is more to racism than we, even as White liberals, realize. As a Black woman and mother, the woman in the audience knew and understood much better than I what I am talking about in these stories.

Fortunately, she picked up on my discomfort and didn't wait for me to talk. Instead, she kindly started advising me that eventually I will be better able to cope with the racism as I "got more used to it." She was sitting perhaps twenty feet away from me in the audience, but her warm words embraced me, as if she were holding me. I will always remember that moment of comfort she gave me. Still, I didn't believe her; I didn't think I or anyone could ever "get used to racism." Years later and looking back on that moment, I cannot say I have accepted racism, but the woman was right; learning how to cope with racism is part and parcel of being Black or loving a Black person.

WE ARE LEARNING TO COPE

So I am getting used to it, if that means that I am learning to take the racial discrimination in stride and not let it constantly depress me. I am getting used to it, if that means that I can laugh at some of the ridiculous things that happen to my daughter because of her race. I realized this during an airplane trip from our hometown to Atlanta. My daughter and one of my African American colleagues were traveling with me. We were going to California on business and my daughter was going to fly to Washington, D.C., to spend a few days with relatives. My daughter and I were able to get seats together, but my colleague sat one row behind us. My daughter and she were constantly interacting during the flight and, at one point, the woman sitting next to my colleague suggested that I might be willing to trade seats with my colleague so she could sit next to *her* child.

As we were straightening out that misunderstanding, the stewardess came back to my daughter to check on her. On the flight from Atlanta to D.C., my daughter was logged into the computer as an "unaccompanied minor" and the stewardess wanted my daughter to wait on the plane for an agent to take her to her next gate. I told the stewardess that wouldn't be necessary; I was her mother and would take her to the next gate before I caught my flight to California. Once at the gate, however, I did want an agent to be responsible for actually getting my daughter on the plane to D.C. The stewardess looked at me skeptically and then asked to see my identification. I think asking for my ID was the responsible thing to do, but I wonder if she asked for it because I am White and my daughter is Black. In one short plane ride in midair, at least *two* people openly doubted I was the mother of the Black child sitting next to me calling me "Mom." And we laughed about it!

My daughter also is learning to live with the inequality. When she was seven, she swore she saw the Easter Bunny and described him as seven feet tall, so tall that he had to duck down low so his ears wouldn't get caught in our ceiling fans. When he was done leaving the Easter baskets, she saw him get into his red car with his wife. He said he was on his way to her friend's house. I love listening to her descriptions of things like the Easter Bunny; she is so animated as she tells them. But the best part of the story was when she took hold of my arm, looked me lovingly in the eye, and said, "Now don't be upset, Mom, but the Easter Bunny was white. It's fair, Mom, because last year he was brown with black spots. So it's fair."

I had to laugh; my daughter was comforting me because the Easter Bunny was white. I realized that my daughter was learning to live with racism, not just for her own sake, but that she also was learning how this affected me as well. From her perspective, if there is balance in the world—as reflected in the different races of the Easter Bunny from year to year—she will think the world is fair.

Interestingly, my Black friends and colleagues tell me that I'll become somewhat immune to the racial inequality in society—just like they have. They say they try not to let it bother them anymore because it's so pervasive that they would be immobilized if they dwelled on it. One of my Black friends, a woman, analogized it to sex discrimination. Sex inequality is also pervasive in our society and, as women, we are very aware of it. But, as she pointed out, "I don't dwell on it; it's just there."

So that's the answer, I thought. Racism is just there and I have to live with it but not dwell on it. I can continue working toward racial equality, but I need to become somewhat immune to the pain of racism. That's how people of color survive and that's how I'll survive, too. Still, I wish there were better answers. The professor and lawyer in me focus on finding better answers, as I explore in Part II, particularly chapter 7. Perhaps the only way to cope with racism, however, is through spirituality and I share some of those insights in chapter 8. My hope is for our children. If our children choose to go to the moon, let it be because they are scientists, not because they are exiles from a society that devalues them.

Part II

A MOTHER SUGGESTS HOW TO CROSS THE COLOR LINE

I approach this part of the book with a great deal of caution and humility. In chapter 7 I don my educator's hat and offer my thoughts about the reasons for the current impasse America is experiencing on race issues, fully understanding that I reside in race never-never land; understandably, both Whites and Blacks are skeptical that I have anything valuable to say about race discrimination. Being in two different worlds and not belonging wholly to either one is part of what it means to love across the color line. Although I am lonely on occasion and long to be a part of a "family" that understands the strange world I inhabit, with time, I have learned that it is a blessing to be in my position. My spirituality makes me believe that I have been given a unique opportunity to see different aspects of the racial divide in America and that perhaps by sharing my thoughts with others, they also will develop a better appreciation of the complexities of race.

Humbly, then, I suggest that many White readers will think about race issues in terms similar to the way I *used to think about them* before my daughter and I became a family. By definition, White people of goodwill believe in racial equality. Nevertheless, it will take a leap of faith for most White readers to stay with me through this part of the book to explore how my personal experiences have shaped my educator's views on race to reach the conclusion that goodwill is not sufficient to attain racial equality. Moreover, I don't pretend to have it all right, as readers of color will quickly realize. If I have learned anything from loving across the color line, I have learned never to think that I really get racism. With this understanding, chapters 7 and 8 are offered as an invitation to reflect on the racial divide in America and to talk about race.

7

UNDERSTANDING WHY GOODWILL TOWARD BLACKS IS NOT ENOUGH

HOW GOODWILL FACILITATES WHITES' DENIAL OF RACISM

When liberal whites fail to understand how they can and/or do embody white supremacist values and beliefs even though they may not embrace racism as prejudice or domination (especially domination that involves coercive control), they cannot recognize the ways their actions support and affirm the very structure of racist domination and oppression that they profess to wish to see eradicated.[36]

As the mother of a Black child, at times I am situated in a different position from my compatriots of goodwill. I often move from the spotlight we share as White liberals and feel isolated from them as I live in the shadow of racism. My new vantage point causes me to question the limits of White liberalism, a plea many Black and some White scholars have been making for a long time.[37] Until my relationship with my daughter, however, I did not fully appreciate what they were asking me and other White liberals to do. My commitment to racial equality as evidenced by my goodwill Whiteness seemed to be the best I could offer.

My motherly experiences bring a reality to the scholars' intellectual teachings. Ironically, to understand this, I had to let go of my goodwill persona and accept that I play a part in subordinating Blacks. My goodwill toward Blacks was not good enough to dislodge my White liberalist's views of the struggle for racial equality. Indeed, a difficult lesson I

121

have learned from living with my daughter is that a major, perhaps the greatest, barrier to the achievement of racial equality is White liberals' comfort in being people of goodwill. As Dr. Martin Luther King, Jr., said of "moderate" Whites in his famous "Letter from a Birmingham Jail":

> I have almost reached the regrettable conclusion that the Negroes' great stumbling block in the stride toward freedom is not the White Citizens' "Councilor" or the Ku Klux Klanner, but the white moderate who is more devoted to "order" than to justice; who prefers a negative peace which is the absence of tension to a positive peace which is the presence of justice; who constantly says "I agree with you in the goal you seek, but I can't agree with your methods of direct action" . . . who lives by the myth of time and who constantly advises the Negro to wait until "a more convenient season."[38]

Being a person of goodwill is comfortable because it does not require much more than declaring oneself a nonracist and supporting the theory of racial equality.

Significantly, the community of goodwill includes just about everyone. Except for avowed racists and White supremacists, almost every White person wants to be thought of as a person of goodwill because most White people of goodwill cannot imagine that any of them would act in a racist manner. By definition, people of goodwill are not racist, at least not intentionally, although occasionally their unconscious racism surfaces. For example, the president of a major university, a White man with a solid reputation for racial equality, recently made a racist comment about a newly appointed chancellor of the Board of Regents, an African American. The president publicly apologized for his comment, and the chancellor and Board of Regents allowed him to remain president.[39] Unintentional racism is easily overlooked among members of the goodwill community.

Unconscious racism that never bubbles to the surface plays an especially significant part in trapping people of goodwill in the limits of their own liberalism. As Professors Joe Feagin and Melvin Sikes point out, racism is understood by most White people to be an attitude of prejudice toward Blacks.[40] In contrast, Blacks define racism more inclusively; it is a system of institutional preferences for Whites, resulting from historically ingrained prejudices Whites have against Blacks. White society's general attitude toward Blacks is reflected in the institutional oppression of Blacks, beginning with slavery and continuing today in ways explored in this chapter. Over the last 300–400 years, the subordination has become reified and an elementary lesson children learn is to accept Black subordination and White privilege as "natural."[41]

This observation usually takes goodwill Whites aback, although it should not be surprising. The viewpoint that Whites are "superior" to Blacks is akin to the viewpoint that boys are "superior" to girls. While people of goodwill openly reject both viewpoints, they nevertheless have become well-settled in young children's (and some adults') minds *despite* the efforts of liberal Whites or liberal parents who teach their children that everyone is equal. Still, while liberal parents seem more able to accept the existence of the false viewpoint of male superiority/female inferiority and openly attest to doing the best they can to fight it, liberal Whites are much more suspicious of the continuing existence of the false viewpoint of White superiority/Black inferiority and are afraid to confront it.

This observation helps explain why people of goodwill are disinclined to attribute racial connotations to ordinary, everyday *negative* interactions involving Whites and people of color *as long as the Whites are people of goodwill (people who do not think they have prejudiced attitudes).*[42] For example, the relevance of race to the story of the softball coach is difficult for most Whites to accept. When that story is added to others—the teachers, the airport woman, the poodle owner, the ambulance driver, the barber, and all my daughter's comments about race, the racism becomes apparent. Perhaps readers are less skeptical now than they were at the beginning of the book about my interpretation of events, but moving beyond goodwill and acknowledging the need to actively pursue racial equality is a difficult journey.

In addition to the stories I have told about my daughter, I could write another book about the racism I see in other parts of my life. I want to tell one story unrelated to my daughter that illustrates how much more aware I am of race today than I was only a few years ago. In one of my colleague's classes, as a Black woman contributed to the classroom discussion, one of her White classmates started jingling his keys. The

Black student interpreted the White student's behavior as racist (and sexist); this was the only time anyone had jingled keys in their classroom.[43] Another White student thought the Black student's perception was outrageous and he quickly and publicly disavowed that the jingling was racist. Rather, he insisted the jingled keys indicated that her comments were wasting time.[44]

The incident became newsworthy around the law school and within days, the White student apologized to the class for his insensitivity, which he assured everyone had nothing to do with race. Some students expressed concern that his apology was half-hearted and superficial, which also made its way around the law school, and students talked more and more about both incidents. The student eventually wrote a more serious apology and published it in the student newspaper.[45]

As events unfolded at school, some White students talked with me and expressed their disbelief that the incident had focused on race because they knew the involved White student and they voluntarily vouched for his racial goodwill. They simply could not imagine any connection between his disrespectful behavior and the woman's race.

As I listened to the students' proffered justifications for their classmate's conduct, I was reminded of the fateful afternoon of softball practice and the footrace incident. Although I saw the relationship between the softball coach's behavior and my daughter's Blackness, I was uncomfortable sharing this with everyone around us because I understood that the White parents' goodwill was unlikely to allow them to see the relationship. In the key-jingling incident, many White students responded by denying that the jingling was related to race, and the coach responded to my daughter's accusation that he held her back by angrily denying it and ultimately inviting us to quit the team. The Whites involved in the different situations reacted similarly to restore goodwill comfort consistent with White denial.

At least three significant concerns arise from these observations, although I return to my experience with the coach because it involved me. First, recall how ludicrous it would have been for me to explain to the softball community how race was relevant to the situation; that would have been too intense and somewhat silly because I have learned how difficult it is to talk about race in meaningful ways in situations where the relevance of race is not immediately apparent to most Whites.

On the other hand, a *mere suggestion* by me that race was relevant to the incident also would have been too intense because the discomfort level was already too high. The coach and I were way too angry to carry on a civil conversation and the most important concern for the coach and parents was to maintain the spirit of goodwill, which acted as a barrier to any discussions about race, particularly racism. To me, the incident was all about race, but to the coach and parents, my daughter's Blackness was irrelevant to any interactions between her and other members of the softball community. Consequently, there was nothing I could have said to the softball community that afternoon that would have been helpful to promote racial equality. If anything, I was supposed to say something to restore everyone (but my daughter and myself) to a level of comfort. Whenever I am in the situation of protecting my daughter from mistreatment—with the principal, the gifted teacher, the woman in the airport—I always feel their discomfort and know they would rather I just stop talking about it. Goodwill can be an effective silencer, although I am developing better skills to talk more effectively across the color line. It is an ongoing lesson.

Second, goodwill comfort is important to maintain, causing many Whites to shy away from *any* discussions about race. Even *positive* everyday, interracial interactions receive no open acknowledgment or discussion. People of goodwill who are unable or unwilling to grapple with negative racial feelings stemming from racism also seem unable or unwilling to talk about race even in positive ways. For example, my daughter's Blackness added diversity to the team and diversity is a value many Whites support. Yet the many hours I spent in the bleachers with other parents never resulted in one conversation about race. It is hard to imagine that no one was curious about her Blackness or our racial differences. Admittedly, I could have raised the topic, but my experiences have taught me it is better to wait for others to raise it and some people do. People who initiate conversations about race are less defensive and more open to learning about its complexities.

Increasingly, however, it seems many Whites get stuck in this paradox: How can race be valuable and yet also irrelevant? How can they talk about race in positive ways and avoid talking about racism? The need to remain comfortable about race has caused many White liberals to stop talking about it altogether. This leads to my third concern.

People of goodwill have felt this cognitive dissonance since the 1960s, when both color-consciousness and color-blindness were the ambiguous orders of the day. Specifically, the late President Lyndon Johnson, a person of goodwill, issued Executive Orders to implement affirmative action in federal contracting.[46] He did this partly in response to the growing unrest among Blacks and people of other colors in the early 1960s. Arguably, implementation of affirmative action programs was a minimal response to the vast problem of racism,[47] but it nevertheless promoted more racial equality than before.[48] It also had symbolic significance because it sent a message that even the president of the United States supported racial equality and would strive to achieve it.

Shortly after the Executive Orders, however, President Johnson delivered a speech at Howard University that implicitly called for race neutrality in White society's thinking about racial inequality. Professor Stephen Steinberg suggests an examination of part of President Johnson's speech:

> [E]qual opportunity is essential, but not enough. Men and women of all races are born with the same range of abilities. But ability is not just the product of birth. Ability is stretched or stunted by the family you live with, and the neighborhoods you live in, by the school you go to and the poverty or the richness of your surroundings. It is the product of a hundred unseen forces playing upon the infant, the child, and the man.[49]

As Professor Steinberg observes, "The conceptual groundwork was being laid for a drastic policy reversal: The focus would no longer be on white racism, but rather on the deficiencies of blacks themselves."[50] In this way, individual circumstances became the focus of Black success, obviating a need to notice or value color differences between Blacks and Whites.

The cognitive dissonance people of goodwill feel continues to move them toward color-blindness because they need a way out of the dilemma that says race is valuable but irrelevant. Their need to maintain goodwill comfort is more important than the need to achieve racial equality. This is increasingly more apparent in the last few years, as many White liberals join with conservatives to explicitly abolish affirmative action. If people of goodwill, both liberals and conservatives, can be convinced that adopting the color-blindness philosophy is in individual Blacks' self-interest, then they will support abolishing affirmative action because they believe in racial equality.

Thus, color-blindness is seemingly a perfect solution to the race dilemma faced by Whites of goodwill. It is only imperfect because it is premised on one big myth: the existence of racial equality. White society posits that racial equality is extant throughout America.[51] Moreover, a focus on formal racial equality provides Whites and their supporters with evidence of racial equality. For example, they quickly point out that Blacks and people of other colors have enjoyed opportunities and attained increasing levels of success denied to them prior to the Fourteenth Amendment and during Jim Crow. In this way, not only is White society beyond unspeakable atrocities of slavery and the open condoning of race discrimination by the government as illustrated by de jure segregation, but White society enacted many laws to protect people of color from race discrimination. Antidiscrimination laws such as the Fourteenth Amendment,[52] the Civil Rights Act,[53] and Section 1983,[54] to list a few, are invoked by White society as concrete evidence that it is not racist and that racial equality is a reality. As Professor john a. powell posits, many Whites believe that racism went out with the government's abandonment of explicitly racist laws.[55]

Further, Whites who suggest racial equality has been achieved point to specific instances where Blacks have been successful at attaining powerful positions. They suggest White society is beyond racism because the following events, among others, would not have occurred in a racist society: The late Thurgood Marshall and now Clarence Thomas would not have been appointed to the United States Supreme Court; the military would not have been racially integrated; Colin Powell would not have been chairman of the Joint Chiefs of Staff; graduate schools, medical schools, law schools, and other public schools would not have increased their enrollments of people of color. In a racist society, none of these phenomena would have happened. A few illustrations of Whites' efforts to promote racial equality, coupled with an example or two of instances where individual Blacks have excelled, are taken as absolute evidence that racial equality has been achieved.[56]

Given this need for people of goodwill to believe that racial equality has been achieved because this makes them comfortable, it also becomes easier to understand the influential forces of "semantic infiltration."[57] This is a rhetorical device used by politicians, scholars, and other people and involves "the appropriation of the language of one's political opponents for the purpose of blurring distinctions and molding it to one's own political position."[58] As long as racial equality has been achieved, then people of goodwill will be supportive of concepts like color-blindness and they also will be more sensitive to cries of "reverse discrimination" because they do not like to be unfair to *anyone*. Even the United States Supreme Court has sanctioned the use of this term *reverse discrimination,* holding that Whites cannot be discriminated against on the basis of their race.[59]

By sleight of hand, many White people of goodwill conflate the apparent absence of intentional racism in their goodwill communities, which they helped eliminate as civil rights advocates, with the existence of racial equality in American society. The general disappearance of intentional racism in their goodwill communities was replaced simultaneously by racial equality in their minds. Moreover, the focus on individual success by Blacks obviated any need for them to confront their support for institutional racism, the systematic subordination of Blacks throughout society. Concurrently, many White people of goodwill metamorphosed from active civil rights advocates who thought they did lots of good to passive people of goodwill who think they do no harm. For example, only a few White educators are concerned about the disproportionate number of Black students in special education classes and the concomitant problem of the underrepresentation of Black children in gifted classes. That this transformation from racism to equality did not happen is at odds with goodwill comfort and is denied.

Moreover, the idea that racial equality has been achieved is necessary to goodwill people because this is the very ideal that gives them their identity. If a few Blacks become members of an otherwise all-White club, that is proof that racial equality exists and they are no longer obligated to fight for it. Because being a person of goodwill is largely attitudinal, obtaining meaningful integration throughout society is not necessary to their identities as racial egalitarians.

In everyday life, the color-blind philosophy works as follows in goodwill communities. When a company hires its first Black chief executive officer, many people of goodwill are unlikely to see this as a step toward racial equality[60] and a cause for celebration for two possible reasons. On the one hand, some Whites posit that the candidate was hired *only* because he was the most qualified candidate; his race was irrelevant in the selection process because *racial equality is already here and the competition was color-blind*. On the other hand, if the company had an affirmative action policy, many more Whites increasingly posit that the candidate was hired *only* because he was Black, which was unfair to the White candidates because *racial equality is already here and the competition should have been color-blind*. Conversely, when the company passes over the Black candidate and hires another White chief executive officer, people of goodwill do not have to attribute the choice to racism and have cause for concern *because racial equality is already here and the competition was color-blind*. The White candidate was hired *only* because he was the most qualified candidate; his race was irrelevant in the selection process. Whites who support this view are particularly persuaded of it if the White candidate was hired *despite* the company's affirmative action policy and its deviation from a color-blind philosophy.

Thus, color-blindness seems to offer a way out of the "race is valuable but irrelevant" dilemma that perplexes people of goodwill. Specifically, they are most comfortable not talking about race and succeed in avoiding such discussions so long as the world operates under their view of color-blindness. Correspondingly, they are less reluctant to talk about race in instances where they believe the color-blind principle is violated, as they think it is in affirmative action. Whites of goodwill do not feel any dissonance between their support for racial equality and their opposition to affirmative action because, from their view, racial equality has become the norm and affirmative action jeopardizes it.

HOW WHITE DENIAL PROMOTES BLACK SKEPTICISM

As most of White society tries to relax in the easy chair of denial, most of Black society increasingly is agitated about the persistent inequality. Justifiably, Blacks are skeptical about White society's commitment to racial equality and as White denial sets in, Black skepticism grows. Consider life in America from Blacks' viewpoint. First, as a factual matter, a focus on formal racial equality reveals that inequality continues to be the norm. The American Dream is held out as a promise of equal opportunity for success and economic prosperity for all members of society. Most people of color understand that the promise is largely an empty one, as visions of their success and economic prosperity fade into the distance, along with White society's memories of slavery and, more recently, Jim Crow's institutional segregation.

For example, White Americans average approximately twice the income of Black Americans and are over two times more likely to live in a family with an income exceeding $50,000.[61] Moreover, Black Americans are unemployed at over double the rate of White Americans and are nearly three times more likely to live in poverty.[62] Current sociological studies report that "95% or more of top positions in major economic, political, and educational organizations are held by White men."[63] Since *Brown's*[64] promise that the government would ensure that children of color receive public school educational opportunities equal to those available to White children,[65] not only do public schools remain largely involuntarily racially segregated,[66] but the economic disparities between public schools that are populated predominantly by White children compared to those populated predominantly by children of color remain grossly unequal.[67] As Andrew Hacker writes, our post–Jim Crow society remains largely divided along color lines, where Whites and Blacks live separately and unequally.[68] Thus, juxtaposed against the promise of inclusion and equal opportunities for everyone is the reality of exclusion and denied opportunities for most Blacks and people of other colors.

More progressive thinkers posit that the struggle for racial equality in the context of formal equality is misguidedly narrow. Not only is the promise of formal racial equality an empty one, but it has done little, if anything, to dislodge Western imagination—colored and White—from a racist political agenda that is premised on White supremacy, the heart of institutional racism.[69] The concept of institutional racism often needs clarification and the definition offered by Stokely Carmichael (former chairman of the Student Nonviolent Coordinating Committee [SNCC]) and Charles Hamilton (a professor of political science) in their book *Black Power* is informative. The following passage distinguishes between individual and institutional racism:

Racism is both overt and covert. It takes two, closely related forms: individual whites acting against individual blacks, and acts by the total white community against the black community. We call these individual racism and institutionalized racism. The first consists of overt acts by individuals, which cause death, injury or the violent destruction of property. This type can be recorded by television cameras; it can frequently be observed in the process of commission. The second type is less overt, far more subtle, less identifiable in terms of *specific* individuals committing the acts. But it is no less destructive of human life. The second type originates in the operation of established and respected forces in the society, and thus receives far less public condemnation than the first type.[70]

The authors continue and provide a concrete example of the different kinds of racism:

When a black family moves into a home in a white neighborhood and is stoned, burned or routed out, they are victims of an overt act of individual racism which many people will condemn—at least in words. But it is institutional racism that keeps black people locked in dilapidated slum tenements, subject to the daily prey of exploitative slumlords, merchants, loan sharks and discriminatory real estate agents. The society either pretends it does not know of this latter situation, or is in fact incapable of doing anything meaningful about it.[71]

Naturally, the voices of Whites who focus their concerns primarily on institutional racism are even less likely to be heard by White society or by their moderate "formal equality" allies of color. Thus, in addition to disagreeing on the question of whether formal racial equality has been achieved, most Whites, including goodwill Whites, also disagree on the question of whether institutional racism exists.

In *Shades of Freedom,* Professor Leon Higginbotham (former federal judge) explores the precept of White superiority and Black inferiority as the underpinning for institutional racism.[72] This precept not only functions to prevent formal racial equality, but it also prevents any kind of racial equality. By definition, the precept posits that Blacks are less talented and capable than are Whites as a matter of biology, a theory popularized by Dr. Samuel George Morton in the nineteenth century.[73] Although largely discredited by the 1930s, this theory occasionally rears its ugly head. For example, in 1994, Richard Herrnstein and Charles Murray wrote *The Bell Curve,* a book that promotes White superior intelligence compared to other races, including Blacks.[74]

Professor Steinberg offers an explanation for this theory's resurgence only a few years ago. Specifically, he suggests that a focus on native intelligence is yet another way of shifting discussions about institutional racism back to individuals. Just as the debate about racial equality in the 1960s shifted from institutional barriers in housing, jobs, and education to individual Black poverty, the current debate has shifted from the same institutional barriers to individual Black merit.

A dramatic indication of the vitality of the precept of White superiority and Black inferiority is seen in the anti–affirmative action movement. At the time affirmative action policies were implemented in the 1960s, any person of color or White woman who was hired by a public employer or admitted to a public university probably was a beneficiary of affirmative action: "but for affirmative action, the Black person or the White woman would not have been hired or admitted." White society's enduring attachment to Jim Crow segregation and its concomitant resistance to integration indicated that without the nudge from the government, public employers and universities would not have taken steps on their own to desegregate their environments on the basis of race or sex.

Unfortunately, the initial purpose of affirmative action, to promote Blacks' equal citizenship,[75] has become lost in the focus on merit. Again, through the use of semantic infiltration, anti–affirmative action activists successfully changed the focus of affirmative action so that some people think it is synonymous with "lowering standards." Shifting the discourse from equality to merit suggests the two are mutually exclusive and plays off the beliefs held by many Whites in the inherent inferiority of Blacks, although the rhetoric of this "new racism" is meant to disguise the message.[76]

Consequently, people who are hired by public employers or admitted into public universities as affirmative action beneficiaries are stigmatized by the negative connotation given to affirmative action. Rather than their addition to public workforces and school programs being viewed as positive steps toward eliminating institutional racism, consistent with the struggle for racial equality, their presence in public programs as beneficiaries of affirmative action is viewed as a negative step backward in America's struggle for national excellence. Couching the objection to affirmative action in the language of "lowering standards" is not as overtly racist as the language used by Chief Justice Taney in *Dred Scott,* in which he reduced Black human beings to pieces of property,[77] but the derogatory message conveyed by the precept of White superiority and Black inferiority in both contexts is equally clear.

Naturally, goodwill Whites resist discussions about institutional racism. Even if they were willing to acknowledge it, they would vehemently object to a characterization of their anti–affirmative action position as promoting institutional racism because it is at odds with their goodwill identity (self-proclaimed nonprejudiced) and also violates the spirit of goodwill because it makes them uncomfortable. In their minds, affirmative action can be abolished, not because they (consciously) think it jeopardizes the quality of America's public employment sector and schools, but rather because they believe in the precept of color-blind equality: the best candidate should win and does win and race has nothing to do with it. As long as sophisticated discussions about institutional racism fall on deaf White ears, Black skepticism makes sense.

Finally, Black skepticism is justified because White society does not even seem to be trying to understand racism. Not only is this evidenced by the prevalence of White denial throughout society, but it is also premised on the reality that Whites can never know the full effects of racism. Regardless of a White person's empathic skills,[78] the person's Whiteness alone largely insulates him or her from racism's harm. Many Whites may think this limitation excuses them from putting their best effort into the struggle.

Moreover, glimmers of hope for ending racism fade quickly if racism's demise depends on Whites' abilities to empathize with victims of racism to a degree where they are moved to repudiate their White privilege. Justifiably, Blacks wonder why any White person would voluntarily repudiate privilege. After all, if Whites were inclined to be so "altruistic,"[79] what are they waiting for? In the next chapter I offer suggestions on this point, but briefly want to highlight here that repudiating privilege is not altruism but rather is premised on correcting a wrong: the privileges associated with Whiteness were borne out of the enslavement and dehumanization of Blacks. Today's Whites may not be responsible for the "sins of their fathers," but neither should they be able to benefit directly from their inheritance of their fathers' White privilege at the continued expense of Black equality. Rather, the act of repudiating White privilege is a necessary step toward equality. Still, Black skepticism warns that the notion that a White person would repudiate his or her White privilege seems too good to be true.

Thus, it is reasonable for Blacks to be skeptical of the sincerity of Whites who profess to support racial equality. In fact, the barriers of White denial, semantic–infiltration tactics, and the anti–affirmative action movement lead to an ultimate skepticism, reflected in the view held by many Blacks and people of other colors that racism is here to stay.[80] Stated alternatively, the continued and persistent de facto involuntary segregation, as evidenced *both* by the disproportionate exclusion of people of color in sharing the American Dream *and* by the perpetuation of "nondiscriminatory" racial subordination, operate to oppress people of color in ways similar to historical institutions like Jim Crow.

This is a difficult lesson for goodwill Whites, who would have to expend immense amounts of time and effort to learn it. Unfortunately, many of them seem unmotivated to study racism, largely because they are in denial, but also because the dominant discourse on race in America reinforces their need to believe that everything is okay. Moreover, their need to believe that racism is history occasionally gets reinforced by prominent scholars. For example, Dinesh D'Souza, a scholar of color no less, posits in his book *The End of Racism: Principles for a Multiracial Society,* that racism *never was a fundamental problem in America* and asserts that even slavery was not a racist institution.[81] In their book *America in Black and White: One Nation, Indivisible,*[82] authors Stephan and Abigail Thernstrom do not deny America's racist history, but throughout their book they do deny that current inequality has much, if anything, to do with racism.

Goodwill Whites need to be jolted out of this stupor on race— dumped out of our easy chairs of White denial we find so comfortable. Even with a jolt, of course, grasping the profoundness of racism on an intellectual level may be inadequate to move some Whites beyond liberalism and into the realm of acknowledging the need to repudiate White privilege and create shared racial space. For example, I wonder if I would have been moved beyond my own White liberalism if I had not become the mother of a little Black girl and fallen in love with her. This thought leads to interesting observations. First, intimate love only occasionally crosses racial lines. For example, in terms of formal relationships, 1992 data report just over one million interracial marriages, of which 246,000 were Black/White couples.[83] With respect to children in interracial families, 1991 data reveal that approximately 128,000 children were born to interracial couples[84] and that almost two million children have parents of different races.[85] This data does not reveal how many Whites were involved in the interracial families, which might consist of all people of color with different races. Nevertheless, the statistics show that a relatively small part of the population enters into formal interracial relationships. Racism is here to stay if White people of goodwill are going to move from their comfortable positions *only if* they fall in love with a person of color.

Interestingly, Alexis de Tocqueville suggests in *Democracy in America* that racial equality between Blacks and Whites can only be achieved by becoming one race of mulattoes: "the mulattoes are the true means of transition between the white and the Negro; so that wherever mulattoes abound, the intermixture of the two races is not impossible."[86] Although de Tocqueville's observation for achieving racial equality is not necessarily premised on love, it is premised on Whites and Blacks developing intimate, even sexual, relationships. Historically, America's legal system was structured to criminalize such relationships precisely to avoid annihilation of Whiteness. Indeed, much of the historical segregation imposed on Blacks was designed to protect the genetic and social purity of the White race by outlawing the mixing of Black and White blood.[87] This is the rationale for the "drop of black blood" caste system throughout America.[88] Recall how my thinking about my daughter's race in filling out the school application form in chapter 1 was heavily influenced by this negative understanding of what it means to be African American in America.

One of the most disturbing stereotypes of a Black man is that of the rapist of the White woman.[89] The 1931 Alabama trial of the Scottsboro defendants illustrates the brutal ways White society responded to accusations of rape by White women against Black men.[90] In Scottsboro, nine young Black teenagers were convicted of raping two young White women on nothing but the women's testimony. As punishment, eight defendants received death penalties.[91] Through a series of appellate court reversals, new trials, more reversals, and more new trials, all of the defendants eventually were set free. Unfortunately, the young men spent an aggregate of "more than 100 years in jail for a crime they almost surely did not commit."[92] The Scottsboro defendants, of course, were not alone in being the target of White society's rage at the prospect of Black men raping White women. As Edward Lazarus reports in his book *Closed Chambers*, "of the roughly 450 Americans executed for rape between 1930 and 1960 almost 90 percent were black."[93]

In reality, most rape is intraracial. "Seventy percent of black rape victims were raped by blacks, and 78 percent of white rape victims were raped by whites."[94] Moreover, the persistence of the myth of the Black rapist has masked the reality and ugliness of the White master raping his Black women slaves—a largely untold story in White American history. Significantly, the myth also masks the story of the modern Black victim by rendering her invisible in discussions about male power and female subordination.[95] As Professor Cheryl Harris observes: "The archetypes of the slave and the mistress were ideologies of womanhood that functioned not simply to describe reality, but to represent social relations in a way that legitimized and normalized racial and sexual domination."[96]

Moreover, White society also found it unconscionable that a Black man and a White woman (or a Black woman and a White man) would have a voluntary intimate sexual relationship. For example, antimiscegenation statutes that imposed criminal sanctions on Blacks and Whites who married each other were not held unconstitutional until the late 1960s—only thirty years ago.[97] The idea of interracial marriage continues to arouse negative sentiments of almost 15 percent of White Americans, who favor making interracial marriage illegal.[98] Many Blacks also oppose marriage with Whites, viewing such unions as a threat to Black unity.[99] My daughter and all mulattoes present special challenges for many people who condemn interracial Black/White relationships. Naturally, falling in love with a person of color does not mean a White person *will* understand racism or be motivated to help end it.[100]

The parent–child relationship involves a different kind of love from that of romantic partners, but it also is characterized by a power imbalance[101] that is magnified when the parent is White and the child is Black because of historical and persistent racial subordination of Blacks by

Whites. The concern that interracial love is inadequate to overcome racism largely shapes the debate about interracial adoptions. Many Blacks oppose adoption by White parents of Black children because they see such adoptions as inevitable "cultural genocide."[102] That is, most Blacks understand the limits of White liberalism; no matter how goodwilled the prospective White parents are, they are not able to fully appreciate the significance of being Black in America.[103]

Thus, arguments against transracial Black–White adoptions rest on an assumption that it would not be in the Black child's best interest to be raised by White parents who have a limited understanding of racism and who cannot teach the child to value his or her racial and cultural identity. Moreover, White parents who believe in color-blindness and knowingly teach their Black children to assimilate into White culture jeopardize the existence of the Black community by altogether undermining the importance of race and culture to the child's identity.[104] This is not in Black society's best interest, either.

Supporters of transracial adoptions posit that policies that prevent interracial adoptions also are problematic and discriminatory.[105] People who hold this view argue that it is better for a Black child to be placed in a permanent home with White parents than it is for the child to be moved from foster home to foster home awaiting adoptive Black parents.[106] Significantly, there are many more Black children available for adoption than there are Black adults willing to adopt them.[107] Finally, supporters of transracial adoptions also emphasize that studies consistently report that Black children raised in White families fare as well as adopted children raised by same-race parents.[108]

As an adoptive White mother of a Black child, I am caught in the middle of the national discourse on interracial adoptions by White parents of Black children. As a mother, though, the debate is moot for me: my daughter and I are a family and to separate us now would do inexplicable damage to both of us. Ironically, the state allowed us to become a family because we were both "imperfect" in its eyes. I was "imperfect" because I was unmarried; she was "imperfect" because she is mulatto. Our deviations from patriarchal and White supremacist values brought us together.

As a scholar, however, the debate continues to intrigue me, although my motherly experiences influence my theoretical analysis. My increased knowledge about racism from loving across the color line informs my theoretical position on interracial adoptions *in two limited and narrow ways.* First, my daughter would benefit from having a Black parent in her life. Professor Twila Perry's suggestion that a Black child raised by White parents does suffer some loss comports with my growing awareness of racism.[109] Specifically, and I am speaking only for my family situation based on what I have learned, I think my daughter suffers from the absence of racial connectedness between herself and a Black parent. A Black parent would be able to understand her pain of racism in ways that I still cannot articulate. Perhaps this deeper connectedness would empower my daughter in ways I do not understand. Coincidentally, she seemed destined to have a White mother, which would have been the case if her biological mother had decided to raise her. Her foster parents and their children also were White.

The second lesson I have learned about interracial adoptions from my position of love across the color line I want to briefly mention here, because I develop this idea in chapter 8. Specifically, I think that my love for my daughter has enabled me to feel an emotion that is more powerful than empathy. I call this emotion "transformative love," because my love for my daughter and my empathic feelings for her and all people of color have caused me to feel the harm of racism in ways that my empathy and love alone did not. This new emotion is transformative for me because it has allowed me to feel racism in a way that helps me understand that experiencing it is not an intellectual exercise aimed at trying to imagine racial pain. Significantly, I think transformative love can happen openly in relationships that challenge institutional power imbalances, relationships like the one I have with my daughter. I feel transformative love precisely because of the intimate and loving relationship I have with my Black daughter as her adoptive White mother.

From my dual mother–scholar perspective, then, I think both sides in the adoption debate have meritorious arguments. There is no empirical way to measure the loss a Black child suffers from being raised by White rather than Black parents. Nor is there any empirical way to evaluate whether the quicker permanent-White-home placement choice outweighs the waiting-for-Black-parents choice. Yet to be explored is this new concept of transformative love, which may be a "positive" aspect of transracial adoptions when they do occur, as it seems they will.

Given this uncertain debate, recent federal legislation governing transracial adoptions struck a balance by outlawing mandatory same-race adoptions but allowing agencies to deny placement of Black children with "racially or culturally insensitive" White parents.[110]

Thus, although I have always espoused positive color-consciousness because I have always "seen" race and think racial differences are valuable, my development from being a person of goodwill to being an advocate for repudiating White privilege and actively abandoning White racism has taken years and is an ongoing process. My life consists of almost daily lessons on racism and race relations, which the stories in Part I are meant to demonstrate. My experiences have taught me a valuable lesson: in addition to reading about racism on an academic level, one must also take deliberate steps to learn about practical, day-to-day effects of racism and White society's denial of equal citizenship to Blacks. Even if people of goodwill do the former, my guess is they do not do the latter.

Racism is intellectually and practically difficult to fathom for most Whites. White denial absorbs most thinking about race among Whites, who increasingly posit that racism is history. Some Whites think formal equality has been achieved; many reject the nondiscriminatory racial subordination theory; and yet a third group of self-proclaimed White supremacists do not believe in racial equality at all. An intellectual grasp of racism may be insufficient to enable most White liberals to understand that repudiating their unearned racial privilege is necessary to end Black subordination and achieve racial equality. Simultaneously, Black skepticism grows as most people of color believe racial equality remains elusive, either because formal equality has failed or because of the more systemic problem of institutional racism that results in their persistent racial oppression. Not surprisingly, this talking at cross-purposes has resulted in an angry racial divide on fundamental questions of racial equality.

HOW WHITE DENIAL AND BLACK SKEPTICISM FEED A CYCLE OF RACIAL ANGER

Racial anger is worth studying because it is an emotion that directly jeopardizes White society's comfort zone and concomitantly manifests deep frustration among Blacks at White denial that racial subordination persists. My experience is that anger seems to lie just beneath the surface of almost every interracial interaction or discussion about race, particularly if the interaction or discussion takes place with a pre-existing underlying tension. Being aware of and sensitive to racial differences minimizes the possibility that any negative racial feelings (even unconscious ones) will exacerbate existing angry ones.

For example, the footrace incident evoked many feelings, but certainly anger was a driving force behind the exchange. My daughter was mad at the coach, he was mad at her, I was mad at him, and he quickly got mad at me. Moreover, my daughter's Blackness and the coach's and my Whiteness were relevant in evaluating our behavior toward each other. Consider the incident from my daughter's and my perspectives. An eight-year-old little Black girl cries herself to sleep because she believes with all her heart that her White coach held her back in a footrace with a White teammate. Moreover, she does not understand why the coach was angry at her for expressing her feelings and insisting that the coach allow the girls to run yet another race but a fair one. Nor does she understand why the White adults witnessing the event remained silent in light of her protests. How could they remain so dispassionate when she felt such turmoil that she dropped to her knees in pain and cried at the unjust way she had been treated? It is impossible to ignore racial differences in any relationship, but this may be especially true when an interracial interaction is characterized by negative feelings. When a person feels mistreated by a person of a different race, it is reasonable for the victim to think the mistreatment had something to do with race.

Perhaps my daughter was too young to articulate the racial dynamics involved in the footrace incident, although she has articulated on occasion how she feels devalued by Whites because she is Black, as revealed by several other stories in this book. Like most Blacks, my daughter constantly is aware of her Blackness and was sensitive to being the only Black child on the team. As her mother, I also am constantly aware of her Blackness. How could she not wonder if her Blackness turned the coach against her? I wondered.

Now I try to imagine the incident from the coach's perspective or the perspective of any White person of goodwill. It is reasonable to conclude that the White person was aware of Mary's Blackness during the angry exchange. This is a realistic conclusion because White people of goodwill consciously try not to be racist, a goal that generally requires maximum effort in an angry exchange with a Black person. How could the coach not wonder if we (or at least I and perhaps the other White adults) were thinking he was racist? And if he did wonder about this, it probably would have caused him to be angrier or more defensive than he would have been with a simple accusation of unfairness that could more easily have been seen as a misunderstanding.

Thus, from both perspectives, race was at the forefront of the angry exchange. Although none of us ever mentioned it, I knew the exchange had an element of racial anger in it. I suspect the coach knew it as well on some level of consciousness, even if he was not fully aware of it.

The footrace incident is a small example of racial anger but nevertheless is significant. As Mary's mother, I am concerned that she will build up resentment toward White society at the injustice she endures. Like most types of anger, racial anger does not appear suddenly but rather festers over time. In a larger context, Professor bell hooks writes that much of the current rage felt by African Americans and other people of color about the absence of racial equality in society centers around White society's denial that ours is a White supremacist society.[111] Continuing, she admonishes, "The danger of that denial cannot be understood, nor the rage it evokes, as long as the public refuses to acknowledge that this is a white supremacist culture and that white supremacy is rooted in pathological responses to difference."[112] The reality of pervasive racism against Blacks throughout society, including seemingly small incidents, supports Blacks' accusations that unfair treatment is race-related.

Understandably, any human being who is persistently subordinated and oppressed is likely to object and protest, and justifiably feel angry or enraged. Legal theory understands this individual human tendency, as evidenced by the concept of "justifiable homicide." For example, some criminal defendants charged with murder have been able to avoid conviction on showing that their murderous anger was justified by some action—persistent physical abuse, violence, threats of harm—directed at them by their victims.[113] In 1968, psychiatrists William H. Grier and Price M. Cobbs identified a mental condition they called "black rage,"[114] which has been offered by criminal defense lawyers in American courtrooms to excuse their clients' criminal conduct.[115] Briefly, the defense is premised on psychiatric findings that the constant racial stress Blacks endure can cause them to act out their uncontrollable rage by committing criminal acts.[116] Whether or not one finds merit in the defense of "black rage," its mere existence sociologically is noteworthy. If nothing else, reflecting on it focuses attention on the profound and justifiable frustration White denial causes Blacks. The defense posits that Blacks' pleas to end racism, when met with persistent denial or indifference, can be a highly effective psychological tool to drive Blacks figuratively or literally mad.[117]

In a different context, a relationship between White denial and Blacks' mental health may seem more plausible. White denial can operate as a form (mild or harsh) of emotional abuse with respect to its use with children. Some of the stories in this book reveal the psychological harm racism causes my daughter. The law plays an especially important role in protecting children from abusive adults, including emotionally abusive adults. For example, child abuse legally has been defined broadly to include inflicting "mental injury."[118] Even if White society is unwilling to acknowledge the psychological toll racism takes on Black adults, perhaps it can better understand how racism in its myriad forms chips away at the self-esteem of children of color. There can be no doubt that racism, especially the precept of Black inferiority, is psychologically unhealthy for children.

Moreover, when oppressors ignore victims' protests or otherwise respond with indifference to victims' cries of pain, naturally the victims' rage and frustration will be exacerbated. Individuals who share concerns about subordination may come together and violently protest. Indeed, White America was established out of rage at English laws that denied colonists the dignities they believed they were entitled to as human beings, including freedom of religion, speech, autonomy, and liberty. Life without these and other dignities called for the Revolutionary War. Another example is provided by the Boston Tea Party, a relatively modest but violent protest, reflecting the colonists' outrage at oppressive taxes. Many historical wars and physical engagements exemplify this point. As victims of mistreatment by oppressive governments, White society has often responded with rage, rebellion, and revolution.

Colored rage is to be expected in a society that privileges whiteness over other racial colors. Alexis de Tocqueville wrote, "To give a man his freedom and to leave him in wretchedness and ignominy is nothing less than to prepare a future chief for a revolt of the slaves."[119] Indeed, America has witnessed several significant riots by Blacks and people of other colors in response to racial oppression. The Watts riots in the 1960s illustrate the profound rage Blacks felt about their subordination. Professors Donald Kinder and Lynn Sanders describe the scene:

> In Watts the violence raged unchecked for three days, and three days longer in sporadic eruptions. Blacks looted stores, set fires, burned cars, and shot at policemen and firemen. Before the violence was halted, 14,000 National Guard troops, 1,000 police officers, and more than 700 sheriff's deputies were pressed into service. More than 46 square miles—an area larger than Manhattan—came under military control. In the end, 1,000 buildings were damaged, burned, looted, or completely destroyed; almost 4,000 people were arrested; more than 1,000 were injured seriously enough to require medical treatment; and 34 were dead, all but three black.[120]

Watts was followed by at least 250 more riots in 1967,[121] a forceful message (similar to the one the colonists sent to England) by Black America that it had had enough of White denial, White privilege, and persistent inequality.

Thirty years later, White America is given another Watts-type message in the 1992 Los Angeles riots following the acquittal of the White police officers who brutally beat Rodney King.[122] Professors Joe Feagin and Hernan Vera describe the riots as the worst ones this century: more than 2,400 people were injured, over 50 died, and property worth billions of dollars was damaged.[123] Certainly, the Los Angeles riots forcefully demonstrate that Blacks, Latinos, Asian Americans, and all people of color continue to be outraged by the unequal treatment they receive in America, even though the days of slavery and de jure segregation are over.

Nor is evidence of Black rage limited to examples of violent outbursts. Just as White society resisted Blacks' nonviolent boycotts and marches (remember how they were "pummeled with nightsticks and set upon by police dogs"[124]), it continues to be challenged by modern Black nonviolent protests of racism. For example, Professor Paul Butler suggests as an antidote to the racial inequality in the criminal justice system that jurors should refrain from convicting Black criminal defendants who are accused of nonviolent, victimless crimes.[125] In his opinion, a criminal justice system that is so permeated with racial inequality should be dismantled.[126]

Not surprisingly, Professor Butler's pleas for a revolution in the form of jury nullification have been opposed,[127] even by other Blacks. A most notable critic is Professor Randall Kennedy, who suggests that jury nullification crosses the line of "respectable" tactics challenging racial subordination.[128] Butler focuses on Kennedy's remarks:

> [F]or a stigmatized racial minority, successful efforts to move upward in society must be accompanied at every step by a keen attentiveness to the morality of means, the reputation of the group, and the need to be extra careful in order to avoid the derogatory charges lying in wait in a hostile environment.[129]

Butler questions why Kennedy is concerned with choosing antisubordination strategies that are not upsetting to Whites: "Kennedy's apprehension of how whites would react to widespread black jury nullification leads him to urge blacks to choose tactics, that, unlike nullification, do not offend the white majority."[130]

This exchange between two prominent Black law professors exemplifies the powerful interplay between White denial and White privilege. Butler justifiably is enraged at the profound and persistent racial subordination in America and thinks radical tactics are necessary to snap White society out of its denial. Jury nullification, although radical and controversial to some people, seems modest in comparison to Watts and Los Angeles. Kennedy may be right that this disturbance of White society's rules may result in a heightened protection of White privilege. If Kennedy is correct, he justifiably is worried about making Whites feel even more uncomfortable about issues of racial equality. Recall that the predominant White response to Watts was to turn away from the Civil Rights struggle for racial equality, and Watts may actually signify the beginning of White society's belief that (enough) equality has been achieved.[131]

Certainly, Watts, Los Angeles, and jury nullification illustrate that White society is not a good listener to Blacks' cries of foul. White America's reactions to Blacks' pleas for equality resemble more those of the British monarch than they do the freedom-seeking colonists who would have appreciated an empathic ear, especially if resolution of their conflicts could have avoided a revolution. Rather than responding to the problem of increasing anger in colored communities with reflection, compassion, and empathy, however, White society uses its privilege to maintain its comfort by creating its own protests as a reminder and insistence of its view that (enough) race equality has been achieved. A specific example is provided by White society's outrage at the Los Angeles riots and what it interpreted as a barbaric "eye-for-an-eye" beating of Reginald Denny by Black rioters. Professor Juan Perea's analysis is insightful: "Reginald Denny's beating created possibilities for certain artificial and misleading symmetries: Even if the Los Angeles police were out of control, so were the black rioters; a black victim is matched by a paired white victim."[132]

Three years later, a jury of nine African Americans, two Whites, and one Hispanic acquitted O. J. Simpson of murdering Nicole Simpson and Ron Goldman.[133] To the amazement of most Whites, most Blacks were ecstatic. Professor David Shipler offers an explanation:

> Perhaps the rush of joy after the Simpson verdict came from a burst of empowerment, a sudden feeling that black people could finally penetrate the high walls of the system to make something right. That may also have been a source of much of the white distress—the notion of blacks having power, of blacks wielding their authority as unjustly as whites have wielded theirs. Black violence and black power seem part of the same continuum.[134]

In White society's eyes, O.J. killed Nicole Simpson and Ron Goldman.[135] The riots and the responses to O.J.'s acquittal dramatically illustrate the different ways Whites and Blacks see race in America.[136]

White society did not respond with like-kind violence to the Los Angeles riots, the Reginald Denny beating, or the O.J. Simpson verdict. Interestingly, within four years of Los Angeles and within one year of O.J.'s acquittal, California passed Proposition 209, making affirmative action illegal.[137] Whether there is a connection between the events is a matter for sociologists or political analysts. My point here is much more modest and does not turn on finding a causal connection. In fact, people of goodwill would not retaliate, at least not consciously. Assuming, then, that Proposition 209 is not retaliatory, then White denial of the problem of racial unrest is perfectly illustrated because passage of Proposition 209 only created more anger and frustration in the Black community as its access to California's public universities was sharply curtailed.[138] If Proposition 209 is related (even unconsciously) to growing White discomfort with racial unrest, then it is clear that not only is White society unable or unwilling to engage in healthy discourse in response to Black anger, but it seems determined to see just how far it can push Blacks' patience to maintain its comfort. Concomitantly, when Blacks explode with rage (Los Angeles) or offer radical theories of antisubordination (jury nullification), White society feels justified in restoring its position of comfort by outlawing policies that promote (some) racial equality and symbolize America's commitment to equality for Blacks.

This view of the anti–affirmative action movement is worth exploring; perhaps there are ways to break the cycle of racial anger. Affirmative action, perhaps more than any other policy on race, keeps society deeply entrenched in an angry debate about racial equality. The two are inextricably intertwined. Whites posit: Equality is here, affirmative action is obsolete. Blacks posit: Inequality persists, affirmative action is necessary. Most Whites are so uncomfortable talking about race that perhaps they think abolishing affirmative action will stop the riots and radical theories and restore their comfortable peace. Simultaneously, Blacks fear that abolishing affirmative action enhances White denial and allows White society to continue to subordinate them. Obviously, eliminating affirmative action will augment the racial divide by placing the burden of managing racial anger on Blacks who will continue to be denied equal citizenship—an increasingly intolerable situation. As the debate rages on, one of the most obvious issues surrounding affirmative action and racial equality is overlooked—Whites and Blacks have not figured out a way to talk constructively about race. In the next chapter, I offer two suggestions White society can take to break the racial impasse and move us beyond our anger. If followed, the steps necessarily take Whites across the color line, opening up possibilities for renewed commitment to the goal of sharing racial space.

8

CROSSING THE COLOR LINE
Two Steps Forward

As this book illustrates, merely supporting racial equality in theory and simultaneously being unaware of or indifferent to the persistent inequality in reality ensures the continuation of the White superiority and Black inferiority precept. Black society's struggle to eliminate the dissonance created by White society's ambivalence about race may well end in violence if White society continues to ignore the dynamics of Black subordination and White privilege. More optimistically, the dissonance can be remedied peacefully if White society actively abandons the precept of White superiority and Black inferiority and repudiates the privileges that attach to Whiteness.

White society can abandon the precept in a variety of ways and in this chapter I want to focus on two significant steps Whites can take toward this goal. First, it is important to lift the taboo on talking about race. People of goodwill need to give themselves room to express their thoughts and ask their questions about race without feeling intimidated or petrified that they will be called racist. Being able to talk about race is necessary to learning about and ultimately respecting racial differences. Second, people of all races should do everything they can to develop authentic interracial relationships. At a minimum, this means being able to care about each other *as human beings worthy of each other's respect, compassion, and support as fellow human beings*. Who knows how much better race relations would be if we reached this basic understanding. Perhaps interracial feelings of empathy, and even what I call "transformative love," might occur with frequency.

My experiences have taught me that taking these two steps is difficult, although several years ago I would have said that I easily had accomplished both of them without much thought. I talked about race in my classes, and I had several Black friends and colleagues whom I loved. Now, of course, it is clear how much I had to learn about relating in authentic ways to Blacks and I share my insights on the importance of *truly* stepping across the color line.

STEP ONE: TALKING ABOUT RACE

Creating Safe Places to Talk about Race

When the coach held my daughter back, I did not think he acted in an intentionally malicious way toward her *because she is Black,* although I do wonder if he semiconsciously knew what he was doing. With a few exceptions, I do not think my daughter's teachers purposefully devalue her Blackness or consciously teach racial inequality in their classrooms. The woman in the airport and the ambulance driver probably didn't think about the racial harm they caused by identifying my daughter as a thief or a drug addict. In fact, the stories throughout this book are not told as tales of evil acts of cruelty or disregard for my daughter's feelings, and my purpose in sharing them is not to point an accusatory finger.

Rather, my goal in this book is to suggest to other Whites of goodwill that most of us have a tendency to deal with race largely on an academic or intellectual level—when we deal with it at all. Significantly, in almost every racial incident involving my daughter, there was little, if any, discussion about race. I share responsibility for this, because I often simply do not know where to begin or how to respond to the unfairness my daughter experiences. I also know that if I try to confront the racism I witness, other Whites will be even more overwhelmed than I usually am and I expect they probably will get angry at me and my daughter. Once an element of anger enters into a relationship, it becomes even more difficult to reach common ground and come to an understanding about the event that just happened. The modus operandi of people of goodwill is to avoid conflict and maintain peace.

Obviously, this book is about how I am learning to talk about race and racism, without being accusatory or self-righteous, but the journey has been difficult. An incident in one of my classes several years ago highlights how intimidated I used to be about talking about race even in an academic setting where race was the topic. The story also highlights the conflict I felt as I tried to maintain my balance both as a White professor of a predominantly White class with two Black students and as a White mother of a Black daughter.

"SLAVERY IS IMMORAL AND WRONG."

Several years ago, I began a discussion of racial equality in Constitutional Law, a class of over one hundred students, with the comment, "Slavery is immoral and wrong." I thought my premise was a noncontroversial, clear statement of the basic starting point for studying the principles of equality under the Constitution. To my amazement, however, a White student raised his hand, objected to the comment, and accused me of imposing my values on the class. I can still hear him asking, "What gives you the right to impose your values on this class?" Although phrased as a question, he was indignant and his tone conveyed an admonishment, "How dare you. You have no right to impose your values on this class!" Without hesitating, he briefly offered the traditional moral justification for slavery: it was necessary for the success of America's agricultural economy.

"Political correctness" was the hubbub of the day, but I didn't think the student really believed I imposed values or cut off class discussions because I disagreed with particular ideologies expressed by various students; he had been a frequent and willing discussant in many classes. Simultaneously, it was unimaginable to me that he actually believed slavery was moral or justifiable. "You think owning another person is okay? How am I supposed to respond to that? It's so wrong," I thought. Literally, I was dumbstruck; his response to my comment caught me offguard.

As he finished his comments, I knew I had to respond in a way becoming to a bright young professor, not in a way that portrayed me as an emotional woman and mother. There were few women law professors on my faculty (on *any* faculty in the United States) and I felt pressure to avoid all the stereotypes of the irrational, illogical, hysterical woman who couldn't control her emotions. It was hard! My rational view of the world had been hijacked by my heart. I certainly wasn't in the mood to debate the morality of slavery, partly because to do so would have been as futile as an academic debate on whether the earth is really round. Frustrated and out of retorts, I probably would have had to end the debate with the brilliant and definitive last word, "Well, that's just ridiculously wrong!" And good teachers never stoop that low.

Therefore, it was important for me to get off the topic of slavery as quickly as possible because I didn't want to lose face as a professor, especially a woman professor, who let her emotions control her. I felt like a teenager who hadn't yet learned how to coordinate her growing body so she didn't stumble with every step. My daughter and I had been together less than two years and I was only a few loving steps across the color line, just far enough over that line to feel the zing of the student's comment *personally,* but not far enough over that line to be in command of both my mind and my heart. So I tried to cope with the situation on an *intellectual* level and I wanted to turn back into the bona fide person of goodwill who tiptoed around racial confrontations when emotions ran too high.

As my heart and my mind were racing to catch up with each other, I looked up from my notes and saw that one of the two Black students in the class had raised his hand. I never would have called on either one of them to get involved in this discussion involuntarily. I was surprised to see that one of them voluntarily wanted to respond to his classmate, especially since neither of them had spoken the whole semester. I called his name and he asked if he could respond to his classmate. Not waiting for my permission, which he didn't need, he addressed the class.

Speaking with a calm, soft voice, he told personal and moving stories of how slavery had hurt his family and marginalized his race from generation to generation—even up to that day. His voice started shaking and we all knew he was on the verge of tears. When he finished speaking, the silence and stillness gripped the room. In the short time it took this incident to unfold, the somberness in the room had the potential to smother us in a permanent veil of silence. I had to say something to break the spell. Clearing my throat, I managed to say, "I stand by my comment. Slavery is immoral."

Class ended shortly after that and some White students went up to the Black student and offered their support. Although pleased with the show of support, the Black student also looked distraught and emotionally spent. He never said another word the rest of the semester. I wonder how many White students in class that day can still hear the Black student responding to a comment that tore him apart. I'm sure he and the one other Black student in the class will never forget it and probably have told it to their Black friends and families many, many times: "You're not going to believe what one of my classmates said in class . . ." Similarly, that's exactly how I broached the subject with my colleagues: "You're not going to believe what one of my students said in class . . ." Naturally, my colleagues were very curious to know how I handled it, and some of them expressed relief that it hadn't happened to them.

I knew all of us in the classroom that day were uncomfortable, but the reasons for our discomfort were radically different. The White student's comment reflected his indoctrination in the precept of White superiority and Black inferiority; this is what he had learned and he had never been disabused of his beliefs. The perniciousness of the precept is best illustrated in the context of slavery, the most horrific institution ever to exist in America. Yet a White student in the 1990s was not ashamed to justify White society's belief in this precept before his classmates. Perhaps some of his classmates agreed with him, but more likely, most of the White students were uncomfortable with the comment because they had learned, at least, that slavery was wrong even if they probably continued to believe on some (unconscious) level in the precept. Accordingly, the White students' discomfort was attributable to their White classmate's violation of the race taboo in the worst kind of way: he said something openly racist.

In contrast, the Black students were uncomfortable that day because they were publicly reminded that at least part of White society continues to believe in the precept and unabashedly supports it. The one Black student's comments reflected Black society's unrelenting struggle to eliminate the precept and assert the truth that Blacks and Whites are equal. Undoubtedly, the Black students also were hurt by their classmate's comment and there is no adequate way to describe how chagrined they must have felt by the ugly put-down.

Looking back, I know I didn't handle that class very well at all. My fear had come true: a White student made a racist comment and I was called upon to assume my responsibility to address it. I was angry at the student for putting me on the spot and making me, the Blacks, and the other antiracist Whites in the room have to respond to such a ridiculous and emotionally draining comment. Talking about race is one thing; responding to a racist comment is quite another. Ironically, while the White student had broken the taboo, the taboo itself had intimidated me to the point where I had lost confidence that I could respond to the incident without being sure that I wouldn't make things worse.

Years later, and from this side of the color line, I see the irony in my fear. I was afraid that talking about racist comments would only make things more hurtful for my Black students. Little did I realize then that my failure to confront racism did make things worse for the Black students. My avoidance told the Black students that the White student's racist comment wasn't serious, wasn't worth discussing. I might as well have said the Black students weren't important. I might as well have said that I only care if the White students learn in my classes because I won't bother to remedy emotional assaults on the Black students that undoubtedly impair their ability to learn just as they impaired my ability to teach. I was modeling the lesson of White superiority and Black inferiority, certainly not because I believed in it, but rather because I was afraid to talk about the nastiness of racism. My timidity put my own needs to avoid confronting racism above the needs of my students—Black and White.

But that was then and this is now and the struggle is ongoing. I have always been a person of goodwill toward Blacks, but my love for my daughter and my growing awareness of the dynamics of racial inequality have increased my awareness of the need to talk about race and racism. I cannot wait for my heart and my mind to synchronize before I am ready or willing to confront racism; my mind cannot intellectualize the pain and make it disappear. Every Black person knows this. Recall the tears in the Black student's voice as he bravely addressed the class and confronted the racism. Sadly, I suspect that few, if any, of the White students truly understood what the Black students were feeling in class that day, an observation I feel confident to make because of the last nine years with my daughter. Comments like those of the student affected me in a new and different way. The insults are not abstract anymore; they are deeply personal. Equally sadly, little did I know then that as my journey across the color line spanned more and more years, the hurt of racism would only get deeper and deeper. A White person of goodwill simply cannot fathom racial pain.

This significant difference between Blacks' and most Whites' understanding of racial pain should not be an impediment to Whites' willingness to talk about race and move closer to the color line. While it is not easy or pleasant for many White people to come to grips with their own negative feelings about race or with their limited knowledge about it, we can and should encourage each other to talk about race. I have learned that it is okay to discuss race because I do not have to worry that I will make mistakes or be misunderstood. I make plenty of mistakes and I am often misunderstood! We all struggle with this and it is unlikely that any of us will truly understand racism. The more we talk about race with each other and with our children, however, the more likely we are to cross the color line. If we step across the color line, we also will understand race and racism much more than we do if we stay on the White side of that line. Indeed, crossing the color line is essential to understand and be motivated to ameliorate racial pain by fighting for racial equality.

BACK TO THE DINNER TABLE

Recall the story about my father's army buddy who used the "N" word at the dinner table. At the time, I didn't speak up and confront his racism because my parents are hard of hearing and I would have had to repeat the insult over and over again before my parents would understand what was going on. Instead, I slipped into the kitchen and ate with the children.

On reflection, it is probably better that I didn't confront our guest because I was too angry at the time and I would have been accusatory. By leaving the room, I was able to let him know that I had been insulted, but it also gave me some time to think about how to respond to him in a meaningful way that might bring him closer to the color line rather than frightening him further away from it. As I was contemplating this, I received an apology from him in the mail and it became clear to me how I could respond to him in a positive way.

I thanked him for the apology and told him that my parents had not heard what he said and that I had not mentioned it to them. And I hadn't. Consequently, there was no reason for him to be embarrassed to see my folks whenever they were visiting my home and I reassured him that he and his wife were welcome. That Christmas, I received a Christmas card from him, and my daughter and I reciprocated. On my parents' next visit, he invited my parents to visit his home. As far as my parents knew, this made perfect sense: my house, his house. Next visit, my parents will expect them to come to back to my house. Our exchanges left the way clear for him and his wife to return to our home. Significantly, if they do visit us again, they consciously will be choosing to cross the color line. Undoubtedly, they will have interactions with my daughter and will treat her with respect. What better way for them to understand race and begin to shed some of their racism? I am thankful I didn't jump all over him at the dinner table because that would have cut off communication. Now, there is hope that he will continue to learn about his own prejudices and begin to reject them.

CREATING SAFE SPACE FOR OUR CHILDREN

Fulfilling my obligation to teach my daughter to cope with racism *actively* requires me to teach her to value and respect herself as a Black girl. Our lives would be easier if adults of goodwill helped me and other parents of Black children to achieve our goals of raising happy, confident children by *actively* teaching their children not to devalue ours. In addition to parents, teachers play an especially prominent role in a child's life and so I am appealing to teachers everywhere to assume responsibility for helping parents to eliminate the precept of White superiority and Black inferiority in their classrooms.

One of my daughter's teachers is a terrific example of what I mean. She is a young White woman who is sensitive to differences among children and expresses genuine concern for them. It is enormously comforting to know my daughter has an adult ally in the classroom—a teacher who willingly talks about race with the children, a teacher who is *positively* color-conscious. Significantly, her willingness to talk about race extends beyond teaching race and cultural differences; the teacher also deals with the everyday aspects of race that inevitably arise in an interracial environment. As difficult as it is for most White people to confront racism, our willingness to do so reflects our acknowledgment that mediating across the color line is important to healthy race relations. The following stories illustrate the teacher's ability to handle difficult racial situations.

THE DESK INCIDENT

One evening, my daughter told me about an incident that happened at school during the morning's "sharing and news time." One of her classmates asked the teacher if it was okay for the class to talk about religion. As my daughter related this, I wondered how the teacher responded. As a lawyer and professor, I know many lawsuits have been brought against public school officials for teaching religious views in the classroom. According to my daughter, the teacher told the child that those kinds of issues should be talked about at home and not at school. Probably what I would have said since the child's curiosity was abstract and not connected to any disparagement of a child based on religion.

My daughter then raised her hand and asked if it was okay to discriminate against people because of their race. She said "discriminate" very slowly and articulately, almost boastfully, as she knowingly borrowed it from adult language. My ears perked up. "Absolutely not!" was the teacher's response to my daughter. Pleased, I asked, "So did you talk about that with your class?" The following story unfolded before the class, as I paraphrase what my daughter said she told them.

"Bobby tried to get his things from Johnny's desk because he wouldn't give them back. I heard Michael yell at Bobby, 'You have no right going in a White man's desk.' I think this is race discrimination," concluded my daughter.

"Wow!" I exclaimed, trying to collect my thoughts. My mind stuck on the words "White man's desk." This was a nine-year-old White boy talking down to his nine-year-old Black classmate from the position of White superiority. Hard to find a clearer example. At such a young age this lesson had settled into Michael's view of the racial world.

Thank goodness for two things. First, a nine-year-old Black girl had the courage to point out that Michael's behavior toward Bobby was wrong and unacceptable. She openly confronted racism and by doing so, she stood up for Bobby, herself, and all the other students of color in her class, even in the whole world. The Black students were empowered by her example and the White students were challenged to confront their own thinking on the issue.

Second, the White teacher had the courage to support my daughter and assume the burden of following through with my daughter's assessment that Michael had discriminated against Bobby because Bobby is Black. By talking about the incident with all the children, the teacher provided a forum for the class to talk more generally about race and equality issues. This included a discussion about the assumptions of White superiority and Black inferiority that were behind Michael's comments, although the lesson was couched in a way that young children could understand.

By the end of the lesson, the teacher had made it crystal clear that race discrimination would not be tolerated in her classroom. She also affirmed her students' need to talk about race and created a safe place for them to do it. In fact, the teacher's openness to talking about race, especially about racism, is one of the most important lessons she will teach her students from one year to the next.

Inevitably, children's lessons on racism need to be repeated over and over because children learn different lessons outside the classroom and racial conflict will continue to arise in the classroom as a result. Sometimes the lesson of White superiority is taught at home, sometimes in religious settings, and sometimes children pick up on it in movies and television. Sometimes the precept is taught explicitly, but most times the lesson is subtle. Nevertheless, the precept permeates children's environments. Consequently, public school teachers who actively combat racism constantly struggle against the odds that their lessons are lasting ones. I try to imagine how I would have handled the following incident if I had been an elementary school teacher.

WHOSE SIDE IS GOD ON?

Weeks went by after the discussion on race discrimination, and the Black and White children got along fine. One night at the dinner table, my daughter asked me to hold her hands because she wanted to tell me about something that happened at school that day. It upset her so much that she shook when she thought about it. I gently took her hands, gave her my full attention, and coaxed the story out of her.

"Today at lunch, Martin [White] told Richard [Black] that God made White people first. Richard tried to tell him that it wasn't true, but then Richard started crying. That made me cry, Mom. I thought they were going to hit each other so I got the teacher. When we got back to class, we talked about it for over an hour."

"So what did you talk about? How were you feeling during this?" I was curious to know because she still could not talk about it without getting physically upset.

"We talked about respect for other people. It ended up with everybody being friends," she assured me. "But it made me and Richard cry again when we had to talk about it. But it's okay now."

It is regrettable that my daughter, Richard, and the other sensitive children had to suffer through the emotional distress that Martin's comment caused them. I also sympathized with the teacher because she had to ameliorate the harm—again. This is an overwhelming challenge, so overwhelming that many teachers, myself included, would rather not deal with it.

Fortunately, the fourth-grade teacher accepts her responsibility to promote racial equality. She also has the support of a guidance counselor who is trained in teaching young children about differences in people. Together, they talked with the class for over an hour about the fight between Martin and Richard and from what my daughter said, the teacher and the counselor were able to avoid substantive discussions about God! This is a remarkable demonstration of responsible teaching.

Martin and his White classmates will grow up to be persons of goodwill, like their parents. If Martin and the other children take the precept of their racial superiority into adulthood, imagine how they will relate to Bobby, Richard, my daughter, and other Black adults. Unless White children are disabused of their feelings of racial superiority, at best, we can expect that White children of today will become the passive people of goodwill who stay distant "friends" with Bobby, Richard, and my daughter, but who semiconsciously support Black subordination and claim they don't know what all the fuss over race is about. At worst, we can expect that White children who are not taught to value racial equality will be like my former student and unabashedly and publicly promote the precept of White superiority and Black inferiority. Surely, our expectations of our White children should be raised so that neither of these phenomena continue. We can do our part to eliminate the precept by talking with our children about the important subject of race.

To say schoolteachers have their work cut out for them is an understatement. I am encouraged that one of my daughter's teachers accepted the challenge to teach her students about racial equality. My daughter's classroom is typical of classrooms around the country, and teaching children not to be racist is a duty all public teachers share. If White teachers held the tiny hands of their Black students as the students related how hurtful their White classmates' racist comments were, the teachers would know what I and other parents of Black children know: holding their hands doesn't stop the shaking. We have to fully embrace them, hold them tight, tell them it will be okay, *and then do what we can to make it okay.* If we can create safe space that allows children to talk about race, we will be off to a good start. Indeed, taking this first step and talking about race is essential to being able to take the second step and develop authentic interracial relationships.

STEP TWO: DEVELOPING AUTHENTIC INTERRACIAL RELATIONSHIPS

The Current Status of White–Black Relationships

If asked how many times they interact with Blacks, most Whites probably would say "never" or "occasionally." Some will say they have a "few Black friends," but generally, most Whites see themselves distanced from Blacks. For example, many of my White friends, who are typical people of goodwill, do not invite Blacks to their homes for dinner, they do not go to Blacks' homes for dinner, and their neighborhoods, churches, and schools are pretty much all White. Their lack of meaningful and caring relationships with Blacks does not come about because my friends are racist; rather, most of them do not have Black friends.

The general dearth of Black friends in most Whites' lives is probably not due to the lack of opportunity to create friendships. Rather, it probably is due to the negative sentiments most Whites have about Blacks, either consciously or unconsciously. Consider that Whites and Blacks have an overwhelming number of daily interactions. In most of those interactions, the people do not know each other's names; they are anonymous passengers on the bus, in the grocery line, in the lecture halls. How people treat each other even in anonymous encounters, however, can be quite telling about their feelings toward each other. The White person who quickly locks her door as a Black man walks by her car is relating negatively to him. She is telling him that she believes in the precept of White superiority and Black inferiority because she expects him to act violently toward her *because he is Black and she is White*. In her mind, his Blackness alone preordains his criminal nature.

Moreover, Whites and Blacks increasingly share work space and because people spend a lot of time at work, there are an increasing number of opportunities to develop interracial relationships. Rather than take advantage of these opportunities, however, many White workers treat Black workers with disrespect. One of my Black colleagues told me that he is offended by the silent treatment he receives from White colleagues who ignore him in the hallway or at the mailboxes, but who cheerfully greet each other and other Whites. I've attended meetings, conferences, and symposia where White colleagues knowingly made racist comments in front of Black colleagues as if they were trying to provoke and hurt them. Many national news stories suggest that racial tension in the workplace is common. Recall the Texaco executives, all White, who shared their contemptuous feelings about their Black employees during a meeting that was taped.[139] Thus, even when Blacks and Whites know each other and work side by side, most Whites relate negatively to Blacks on a daily basis.

Concomitantly, just as most Whites think they have neutral, if any, interactions with Blacks, Blacks daily grow weary fighting White racism. The struggle is so exhausting that more and more frequently, Blacks talk about how they would rather stay segregated in their own communities where they don't have to interact with Whites. In the last ten years, for example, the emphasis on equality in public schools has shifted from desegregation to economics; Blacks are content to have their own public schools so long as they are funded at equal levels with White public schools. This is a dramatic reversal from the 1954 decision in *Brown v. Board of Education* when the Supreme Court assumed economic equality between Black and White schools, a clear fiction, in order to ask the critical question: Can forced social segregation be equal? The Court's unanimous answer was "no," because the Court believed that "[t]o separate [Black children] from [White children] of similar age and qualifications solely because of their race generates a feeling of inferiority as to their status in the community that may affect their hearts and minds in a way unlikely ever to be undone."[140] Naturally, but without articulating it, the Court's holding also was an indictment of White superiority, the other half of the precept.

In light of *Brown*, Black communities' current emphasis on securing economic equality for their involuntarily segregated public schools is noteworthy. Blacks realize the Court's goals in *Brown* have not and are unlikely ever to be achieved unless America recommits to the value of racial equality. Moreover, and ironically, we also have learned with time that just the opposite of what the Court said in *Brown* is true today. Black children's self-esteem is fortified in Black schools, because the precept that *Brown* tried to dismantle holds fast in predominantly White public schools. By remaining segregated, Blacks escape having to relate to Whites, which is enormously empowering in a White society that constantly treats Blacks unequally. Their segregated communities offer respite from the constant barrage of racism.

Like it or not, then, Whites and Blacks are engaged in relationships, but they are largely disingenuous because they are premised on negative stereotypes Whites have about Blacks, which show a lack of good faith by Whites. More emphatically, this inauthenticity stems from Whites' adherence to and persistent belief in the precept of White superiority and Black inferiority. Simply put, one cannot enter into and maintain authentic relationships that are premised on a power imbalance, particularly an imbalance that is as dramatically unequal as that between Black and White Americans.

Critically important is how the power imbalance is perceived and characterized by young children. Generally, the degree to which children are learning the precept is evidenced by how they treat each other. Recall the story of the Black boy trying to retrieve his property from the

White boy's desk, only to be told by another White boy that he didn't have any business in a White man's desk. Much to my astonishment, I learned that my daughter thinks that Whites actually hate Blacks. Here goes:

"Mom. Explain something to me. There are so many black things in the world. Some people have black hair (she tugs at her own), there are black shoes, black cars. Even the nighttime is black. So tell me. How come with so many black things to hate, White people pick something with feelings? I don't get it."

Her skinny little legs are slipping under the covers as her inquisitive black eyes search mine for an answer. "Can you explain that, Mom?"

The look of bewilderment on her face told me she knew I couldn't explain it. Her question was rhetorical and on some level she knew it had no answer; at nine years of age, she knew it.

"How I wish I could explain that," I tell her, covering up the rest of her with her blanket. "But I can't. It doesn't make any sense to me, either. White people have a lot to learn, don't they? And that's what our book is about, darling. Whenever you are ready and want to, you can write something for it. I'll be sure it gets in."

Most White people of goodwill would not agree with my daughter's observation that Whites hate Blacks. By definition, White people of goodwill "don't have anything against Blacks" and even wish them well. They would deny they dislike Blacks in any way, let alone hate them. Hate simply isn't part of the self-image of a person of goodwill. In this way, White denial allows White society to think it has a neutral, even positive, relationship with Black society. Individual Blacks in individual Whites' lives are distant parts of Whites' semiconscious awareness that there is an institutional race problem in America but it's not *their* problem. In reality, of course, White society's disdain for Blacks occupies a huge space in its collective unconscious White mind. Simultaneously, the disdain and denial wear Blacks out and make them seek safe havens of respite from racism in their own communities. It is no wonder that Blacks want to isolate themselves from White society; I wish my daughter and I could escape the racism, too.

Children, especially children of color, are quick to sense racial tension. A little nine-year-old Black girl deduces that Whites hate Blacks because she knows how White society has treated her in her short life.

All of the stories in this book attest to the reality of her understanding of the world. I bear witness. My daughter and I live, *day by day, hour by hour, minute by minute,* the disdain most Whites have for her and all Blacks. Our experiences affirm the social science research that shows almost 75 percent of all Whites believe in the truth of a negative stereotype about Blacks.[141] Significantly, the White people who hurt or marginalize my daughter are not the skinheads or the avowed White supremacists. They aren't even the "Archie Bunkers"; they are teachers, coaches, airline passengers—ordinary, everyday people in our lives.

Given that Whites and Blacks are in disingenuous relationships defined by White superiority and Black inferiority, the most important word in my suggestion that people of all races create authentic relationships is the word *authentic.* Authentic relationships, by definition, are ones in which the partners are imbued with equal dignity and respect; ones in which the partners are valued for their unique personalities, including characteristics like race and gender that inform the individuals' very identities.

On a most optimistic note, authenticity reflects the quality of children's relationships with all people before the children have a chance to learn biases and prejudices. In fact, to get children to abandon the natural respect they have for each other *as human beings* requires adults to teach them disrespect, bigotry, hatred, and prejudices. Literally, Whites have to deceive children to get them to believe that the paradigm of White superiority and Black inferiority is "natural" or part of "God's plan."

For example, given all the insights on race that my daughter and I have shared in this book, it is remarkable that my daughter continues to have a loving attitude toward individual Whites and with White society. This is an enormously powerful testament to children's basic goodness, because even though she thinks Whites hate Blacks, she doesn't hate Whites. I'm not even sure she knows what hate is, only that it is bad. When she listed the number of black things Whites could hate, it was as if she were offering a solution to the problem of White racism. Translated, here's what I heard my daughter saying: "Hey, I've got it. Why don't we point out to Whites that they can hate these other inanimate things and not hurt anybody and then they can stop hurting Blacks because Blacks have feelings." In her naiveté, she wonders how this simple solution could have escaped Whites. Most important, she has deduced that Whites hate Blacks, not because Whites are evil, but rather because they just haven't figured out how to direct their feelings in a nonhurtful way. She's willing to give Whites the benefit of the overwhelming doubt.

While young children are in their naive and innocent stages of growth, responsible adults enjoy a prime opportunity to foster the authenticity of children's relationships. Most White adults will need to reevaluate their own feelings about race and how they relate to people of color to participate successfully in this effort. As a basic starting point, Whites who want their children and themselves to have authentic relationships across the color line must value Blackness. In addition, individual Whites, even White liberals, must make an effort to explore the roots of their own prejudices, which are deeper than most White liberals think or can even imagine. Speaking from my experiences, the journey of self-reflection is one that I didn't even know I needed to take. Now that I am on my way to truly understanding racism, I cannot express how essential self-reflection is in the struggle for equality. If Whites are willing to do the self-reflection and also are patient and determined to overcome Blacks' skepticism and desire to retreat to safe places, only then will society see the development of authentic interracial relationships. These are difficult and necessary, but not impossible, steps for White liberals to take in the struggle for racial equality. The awareness, coupled with the goodwill, lays a foundation for developing authentic interracial relationships built on empathy and, ultimately, "transformative love." Let me explain.

ON EMPATHY: "DO I UNDERSTAND YOU TO MEAN . . . ?"

Empathy is the ability to put oneself in someone else's shoes to try to understand how the other person sees the world. Developing an empathic understanding of racism is extremely difficult and my personal experiences attest to this. On many occasions, my daughter would be mistreated and yet it would take time for me to come to grips with the racial aspect of the mistreatment. I spent a lot of time second-guessing my judgment and questioning my view of the world. "Was my daughter's race *really* relevant to the coach's treatment of her?" "Is it possible the schoolteacher's failure to place my daughter in the gifted class was simply an administrative oversight?'' And on and on my mind would go. My doubts about racism were situated in my allegiance to White goodwill, a persona with which I strongly identified.

Juxtaposed against my previous doubts is the stark reality of my daughter's experiences. Some of her most poignant insights are worth highlighting as I make this contrast:

At three years of age, she asked, "If black is so special, then why isn't it in the rainbow?"

As a four-year-old, "Don't White children know that everyone has a heart?" "I wish I were White."

Five years, "Can a Black man be president?"

At six years, "You have to be White to get that award." "Who are those guys in the sheets?"

At seven, "I'm going to fly to the moon because it's no fun being dark." "I should wear a video camera so you can see what I have to put up with at school."

As a nine-year-old, "Why do Whites hate something with feelings when there are so many other black things to hate?"

And these are her insights; they don't include the explicit racial assaults: being called a purse thief, a drug addict, God's inferior creation. Moreover, the implicit racial assaults are overwhelming: being held back in the footrace, having White people run away from her, being segregated in the classroom, the presumption by many teachers that she didn't and couldn't belong in the gifted class, being painted pink (White) by the artist, the numerous suggestions that she isn't equal to Whites or to boys, the constant exposure to media barrages that associate bad and evil with blackness, and the list goes on. Indeed, the most amazing point that bears emphasizing is that it took me years to *feel* (not just witness) what my daughter and every person of color feel on a personal, day-by-day basis: racism.

I used to be embarrassed to admit that until a few years ago I did not fully comprehend the depth and pervasiveness of racism. Ironically, now it is less embarrassing to admit that it took me so long to cross the color line and more embarrassing to admit that, until a few years ago, I thought I had already crossed the line many, many years ago.

My "slowness in getting it" doesn't reflect my lack of intelligence or concern for racial equality. Realize that during those eight years, I did fight for my daughter and speak out against the mistreatment. I met with teacher after teacher; I continued to teach and write about racism; I built up her self-esteem by dispelling the myth of White superiority and Black inferiority at every opportunity. It took a long time to understand how pervasive racism is because there is so much denial about it that the denial becomes a part of a White person's psyche—especially with each generation that is further and further removed from the days of slavery and Jim Crow. This is not offered as a justification, excuse, or rationalization for my slowness, but rather as an observation. I went as fast as I could in a White society that tried to draw me into the conspiracy against Blacks in every way conceivable from the day I was born. And my resistance to that pull is a daily struggle.

Thus, I do not want to underestimate the enormity of my suggestion that Whites develop their empathic skills with respect to relating across the color line. On the other hand, I don't want to discourage Whites from confronting the problem and becoming part of the solution, either. Fortunately, becoming antiracists who actively and consciously reject the precept begins with small steps, building on awareness and concern. But mostly it begins with the basic tenet adults learned as children: to respect every person as a human being.

Moreover, because Whites often have few meaningful interactions with Blacks, empathic skills can be learned from experiences that are unrelated to race but that extrapolate to racial contexts. For example, one of my students, a young White man, came to my office one afternoon to chat. It had been over a year since he was my student, but we had continued to work together on a few projects and had a comfortable professional relationship. During our conversation, he shared with me a story about his baby daughter. Within a year of the baby's birth, doctors worried that she might have a debilitating disease. My student told me that the experience with his baby had finally made clear to him what I meant when I talked about the pain of racism. I wanted to hear more.

My student knew some of the stories in this book and he related in my office that afternoon that while he had been moved by the stories, he had never fully believed that Blacks continue to suffer from racism to the extent I had suggested. He sympathized with Blacks and people of other colors who had to endure the harm caused by race discrimination, and he genuinely believed that society would experience less racial tension and develop a greater sense of racial equality if color-blindness became the prevailing theory behind government programs and school admissions policies. What he couldn't imagine is what I meant when I suggested that simply *being Black* disadvantages my daughter in a society that values Whiteness over all other racial colors.

When he personally faced the possibly that his baby might have a debilitating disease, he was forced to try to imagine what his daughter's life would be like as a "different" child, as he described it. He was tormented with worry. How was his daughter going to cope with the inevitable physical limitations and emotional harm that resulted from stares, rejections, and teasing, which would become daily parts of her life? How would other people treat his child? How would he get people to value his child? He related that he finally understood how it felt to have one's child be ostracized and to be powerless, as a parent, to do much about it.

More important, my student was trying to connect with me even though our pains for our daughters were situated in different experiences. My telling of this story is not an invitation to make comparative and qualitative analyses about different types of pain. That seems counterproductive and at odds with the goal of developing empathic skills. Rather, by talking about our daughters that afternoon in the privacy of my office, my student moved closer to the color line and I moved closer to the line separating children from each other because of health differences. His personal painful experience with his daughter, although unrelated to race, enabled him to understand on a deeper level that there is something more to racial pain than he realized when he first heard my stories. He became less suspicious of my stories and more empathic toward Blacks.

The conversation with my student was encouraging. It exemplifies the dilemma White people of goodwill face who want to engage in authentic relationships across the color line but aren't quite sure how to do it. Their discomfort arises because most Whites continue to be suspicious that racial inequality persists, but upon reflection, they also cannot summarily dismiss the reality of racial inequality, because on some level of consciousness, Whites know the truth and they know that Blacks know the truth, too. Consequently, Whites are aware that accepting the reality of racial inequality will be an essential and fundamental understanding of an authentic relationship with a Black person. Accepting the reality of racism, moreover, is only one element of the discomfort that Whites must grapple with if they want to develop authentic interracial relationships. An authentic relationship between a White person and a Black person also is premised on the White person's willingness to talk and learn more about race and racism. Rather than hiding behind White denial, a White person who enters into an authentic relationship with a Black person is making a commitment to help end racial inequality. The authenticity of the relationship is premised on this basic promise.

Thus, the everyday stories like those of my daughter's may move Whites to reflect on areas in their lives where they rely on the goodwill of other people to help them deal with particular situations in their own lives. Although the relationship I had with my student was only tangentially about race, by drawing on his experiences with his own daughter and trying to put himself in my shoes, he better appreciated my role as a mother of a Black child. In turn, his empathic skills allowed him to relate to me in a way that affirmed that part of my identity. Not only did race become an acceptable topic for us to discuss, but it also became an essential aspect of our relationship. As soon as he was able to acknowledge that part of my racial identity that is deeply connected to my daughter, our relationship became more authentic.

Deeper reflection takes the White mind beyond the shocking examples of racism illustrated by the dragging of Mr. James Byrd to his death in Texas and the killing of Isiah Shoels in Littleton, Colorado, and into the more subtle areas of racism that many of the stories in this book reveal. The truth about racial inequality comes very slowly to Whites because we have been so ingrained and invested in the precept of White superiority and Black inferiority. Perhaps just one of the stories in this book will give readers pause and make them reflect on their own views. To be at the "pause" stage is to be closer to the color line. It may take a while for the significance of a particular story to register with the reader, but eventually it will if the reader is open to learning about race. Tapping into that dormant realm of truth is a necessary precursor to eliminating racial inequality, and valuing equality is part of our self-definition as people of goodwill.

THE HUMAN SPIRIT

For at least the six months before my daughter's tenth birthday, I was in a deep depression about the state of racism in America. Unwittingly, I began to withdraw from my colleagues and had trouble sleeping or thinking about anything but race. My obsession with racism overwhelmingly saddened me and I had trouble completing this book because trying to combat racism seemed fruitless.

It may seem ridiculous or naive that I had never taken seriously the possibility that racism might never end, especially given my background as a civil rights law professor. In fact, several of my Black colleagues had written articles in which they suggested this possibility, but I simply didn't want to believe it. It was only within a year of completing this book that I realized that racism will outlive me and my daughter. Notwithstanding this realization, I am optimistic that racism will and can end someday during somebody else's lifetime.

When I look back on those dark months of depression, I wouldn't want to relive them, but I am thankful for them; taking a break from the theoretical struggle to end racism may have been the best medicine for me. Time not spent obsessing over racism gave me more time to spend with my daughter. And there lay my ray of hope. Once I focused exclusively on her and the love we share, I began to see some possible answers to what, at times, seems like an intractable problem.

Two wonderful things happened to me as a result of my depression. First, working to get beyond the depression, I discovered that my experiences with my daughter in the nine years we had been together had evoked in me an emotion more powerful than empathy, but for which there is no word in English. I think this emotion, which I am calling "transformative love," may be essential to achieve racial equality. If that sounds too optimistic, I nevertheless take enormous comfort in this discovery because transformative love provides a spiritual basis for transcending racism—at least on a personal level. This awakening was the second wonderful thing to result from my depression.

TRANSFORMATIVE LOVE

Transformative love,[142] as I mean it, differs from my empathic feelings for Blacks or even for my daughter. It also is different from the "typical" motherly love I have for my daughter. Instead, transformative love combines my empathy for all Blacks with my motherly love for my daughter. Let me try to explain why neither empathy nor typical love alone is sufficient to undo racism.

As I discussed earlier, it is essential that people of goodwill develop their empathy toward Blacks if America wants to achieve racial equality. I have learned, however, that empathy alone may be insufficient to achieve that goal; certainly, my empathy for Blacks, which I have felt all my life, did not evoke this new, more powerful, emotion in me. The primary reason empathy is a limited, albeit important, emotion in the struggle to dismantle racism is because it requires Whites to *imagine* the pain Blacks feel from racism. In living with my daughter and witnessing the mistreatment she receives from Whites, I often feel a variety of emotions that cause me physical discomfort. All loving parents can relate to the torment one feels when one's child is treated unfairly. Yet empathic pain develops *only because someone else is hurt* and witnessing the harm triggers the emotional response.

Transformative love, in contrast, moves beyond racial empathy because it does not depend on Whites' imaginations. A person who experiences transformative love literally *feels* some of the direct pain caused by racism. For example, my depression, stomachaches, anxiety, and many other negative feelings that accompany racism are involuntary physical responses I have because of that social disease. Sometimes I have these feelings without witnessing an ugly racial incident, because racism, including its pain, is part of my life.

Importantly, I am not saying that I *know* what Blacks feel when racism hits them; I don't and I never will. I am saying that I used to think empathy was as close as one could get to understanding another's pain. Loving across the color line, I am feeling something that is deeper and more personal than empathic pain. Ironically, this new feeling, although situated in feeling the pain of racial injustice, is more empowering than empathy when it is mixed with love.

Thus, in addition to my racial empathy, my love for my daughter also was essential for me to feel transformative love. Moreover, the transformative love I feel builds on the "typical" love that I have for my daughter. Focusing on how transformative love differs from typical love is important, because I am not suggesting the former is deeper or more meaningful than the latter. Typical loving relationships like those between parent and child, spouses, siblings, and many other people are extremely powerful. For example, loving parents would sacrifice their lives if it meant saving their child's life. Typical love as I mean it is a wonderful and beautiful emotion.

Transformative love differs from typical love, then, not in quality but in kind. Transformative love is a unique kind of love because it has an opportunity to arise in relationships where there is an institutional power imbalance between the people in the relationship. It may be easiest to explain this in the context of relationships between a man and a woman, which is the most common place for transformative love to develop, and then I'll return to interracial relationships. I also want to use the father–daughter relationship because it most closely parallels my experiences with my daughter, but this analysis can be applied to any relationship between a man and a woman: husband–wife, brother–sister, lovers, or friends.

Naturally, within any loving relationship, the man and the woman probably treat each other with dignity and respect. Nevertheless, as everyone knows, institutional sexism continues to exist despite America's efforts to achieve equality between the sexes. In this way, a loving father who is committed to achieving equality between men and women has an opportunity from living with his daughter to witness sexism on a personal and sustained basis. Whether the father's love for his daughter turns into transformative love depends on how well-developed his empathic skills are with respect to women who suffer oppression because of sexism, and it also depends on how sensitive he is to the day-to-day experiences of his daughter, who combats the precept of male superiority and female inferiority since birth or shortly thereafter. The more empathic and sensitive the father is to his daughter's struggle, the more likely his deep love for his daughter will develop into transformative love.

What does this mean? Transformative love literally wallops the man's sensibilities when he begins to feel the pain of sexism, not just because his daughter is hurt by it, although reacting to her pain lays a foundation for empathy. Rather, transformative love develops because the father understands on a deeply personal level the oppressive nature of institutional sexism. Sexism becomes a part of his day-to-day life, because the father must reckon with it to achieve peace within himself. Naturally, part of the father's need to be at peace is tied to his desire that his daughter be treated equally compared to men, but that is now only part of his motivation in struggling for equality. This is why I call this feeling "transformative," because it causes the loving father to be highly motivated to take personal steps to end the oppressive forces that are hurting his daughter, all women, and now himself.

The steps the father or any loving man takes to contribute to the struggle for equality can be small or large. If we look at the world around us, we see men taking steps that reflect transformative love. For example, within the last twenty years or so, we have seen society acknowledge sexual harassment as a problem of institutional sexism and many men have joined with women to deal with it. Certainly, one goal of these efforts is to protect individual women from being harassed by individual men. More important, however, the larger goal behind the efforts is to eliminate the institutional support for the precept of male superiority and female inferiority. The precept is supported whenever society allows men to treat women as sex objects rather than as human beings who deserve to be treated with dignity and respect. I am persuaded from my experiences loving across the color line that the transformation of parts of society's thinking about the proper role of women from that of sex objects to that of men's equals is occurring largely because loving men are beginning to feel the injustice of institutional sexism and can no longer tolerate it.

Interracial loving relationships provide another fertile ground for the development of transformative love. I know firsthand the power of this emotion. For example, I understand the complexities surrounding Black subordination and White privilege in a way that had not come to me before my loving relationship with my daughter. I understand from living with my daughter that the struggle against racism for a Black person is a constant and unrelenting one. I understand how pervasive racism is. I understand how devastating it is, particularly to Black children.

All of these deeper understandings of the dynamics of racism have led me to transform my view of institutional racism and how to combat it. As an individual White person in the struggle for racial equality, I understand how limited my goodwill toward Blacks is; I understand how limited my empathy is; I understand that typical love for Blacks also is not moving the struggle forward. Only by putting all of the energy of these emotions together is a White person going to be motivated to achieve racial equality, which is premised on White society restructuring itself so that Blacks are treated with equal dignity and respect.

Unfortunately, I also know firsthand how rare this kind of love is in the context of interracial relationships. Most obviously, it is rare because, as I explored earlier, there are not very many formal or informal loving relationships across the color line. Accordingly, transformative love has been slower to evidence itself in the struggle for Blacks' civil rights than it has been to evidence itself in the struggle for equality between men and women. Moreover, transformative love also is rare even in loving interracial relationships because it takes a long time for most Whites' empathy, love, and awareness to come together to overpower the predominant, ingrained beliefs held by White society in the precept of White superiority and Black inferiority.

One might think that my new awareness of the depth of racism throughout America would make me more depressed, given that I now have a much better and more realistic idea of how long and hard the journey toward racial equality is. It also has taken me an enormous amount of time, about nine years, to be able to feel transformative love and to try to articulate it. The magic of this feeling, then, is the hope that it has given me against all odds that racism will end in my lifetime or even my daughter's. Let me explain.

"IT'S A SPIRITUAL JOURNEY, MOM."

As I write the last part of this book, my daughter and I are entering another stage in our relationship and our understanding of race and racism in America that is worth sharing. She is on the cusp of outgrowing her naiveté and learning to grapple *explicitly* with Whites' mistreatment of her as a Black girl in America. Anticipating this, I expected I would have to combat what I thought would be a natural tendency for her to become defensive, angry, perhaps even hateful toward White society.

Many times, in the solitude of her bedroom, what should have been moments of celebration of life's joys for that day and anticipation of what joys tomorrow would bring were moments spent agonizing over unanswerable questions that shouldn't need to be asked by any Black child. Admittedly, there are times when I want to deride Whites in front of her, say something about how mean we can be as a race. But I resist this temptation because I do not want to teach her to hate Whites. Rather, I want to build up her self-esteem and I'm teaching her to situate the problem of racism in the Whites who mistreat her. I want her challenge to be, not one of fighting off anger and resentment, but rather one of finding her spirit and thinking of ways she can help eliminate racism.

She can play a significant role in helping to develop authentic interracial relationships by demonstrating compassion for Whites who put her down. She is learning to value all people as *human beings who are worthy of her respect as human beings* even though they perpetuate the precept. I'm trying to teach her to continue to give Whites the benefit of the doubt and to take the "high road" through life—not in a self-righteous way but in a self-affirming way. The problem of racism is a White problem but she is learning that she also can be part of the solution to the problem of racial tension if she maintains her Black pride and her human integrity. She deserves to be free of hateful feelings so her energies can be used to accomplish positive things. Thus, it takes us less time now than it did a few years ago to get back on a happy track after incidents in which she is mistreated because I now know what role I can play as a White person who loves across the color line.

I often have asked myself how Blacks cope with racism and while I'm not positive how they do it day in and day out, I know that developing a spiritual center is important. About the time I began to articulate my idea of transformative love, my daughter wrote something for the book that resonated with what I was feeling and also with my growing awareness of the importance of spirituality in the daily struggles against unfairness. I have shared the writing of this book with my daughter from the beginning, although it is only as she has gotten older that she has taken an interest in it. I invited her to write something for the book on several occasions, and a few months before her tenth birthday she wrote the following:

My Word to the World

I give you my word that I will stop all racism. I don't care how long it takes, I will stop all racism. It could take 100, 1,000, 100,000,

1,000,000 [years]. I will reach that goal. I could die but I still would reach my goal. I would die and my spirit would go into the right person, and if they didn't reach it before they died, then their spirit would go into someone else. That would go on and on and on until my goal was reached. But I can't reach my goal without everyone's cooperation. I need your help to be able to reach that goal. All you need to remember is that no matter if you're black or white, Asian or American, boy or girl, you are just as special as anyone else in the world. I will stop all racism.

It is worth emphasizing that she was nine years old when she wrote this. By coincidence, just as it struck me that racism would outlive my daughter, she wrote this essay telling me that she knows and accepts this reality. I cannot describe how comforting her perspective on racism is; the healthiest way one can cope with racism is through one's spirituality. Fortunately, this new feeling of transformative love allowed me to hear what my daughter was saying, even though my Black colleagues had said this to me years ago and I didn't believe them. All the time I have spent laboring over trying to find legal ways to achieve racial equality, my daughter has known all along that "It's a spiritual journey, Mom." Laws can ameliorate some racial pain, but true racial equality will be achieved when there is a spiritual transformation in America. My hope stems from finally knowing and understanding this.

Recently, I coauthored an essay in which the other authors and I were asked to try to describe what society would look like without racism—Utopia. For weeks, nothing came to me. That's how impossible it was for me to imagine a life without racism. My feeling of transformative love, my security in my daughter's spirituality, and also my own spirituality, allowed me to suggest in the essay that, although I cannot describe what Utopia would be like, I do know what it means to have "Utopian spaces in my heart." My daughter and I rejoice in our love for each other, in the blessed life we live, and in our hope that more people can experience the profound happiness that comes with loving across the color line.

EPILOGUE

T he evening after softball practice, Mary and I had a long talk about what had happened with the coach. She wanted to know why he was so mean to her. Whenever I hold her, I am taken aback at how small and fragile she is. Her eyes are so black one cannot see her "peeples," as she would say, but their blackness cannot hide the pain and confusion of being mistreated. She still has the innocent face of a young girl, eager to take in all that life has to offer—always expecting the best of everyone. Although she feels the hurt of racism, she is not old enough always to understand what is happening to her and why.

We talked about quitting the team. It was hard for me, as an adult and a White person of goodwill, to imagine seeing any of those people again. I could feel the pull toward comfort; accepting the coach's invitation to quit was alluring. I rationalized: Why should she have to endure his disdain? On the other hand, I have learned from being her mother that I must teach her how to cope with unfairness, because it is too much a part of her life not to confront it. Accordingly, I tried to focus my daughter on the future. I told her that there would be many times in her life when people would try to divert her from her goals. In some ways, it did not matter why the coach did what he did. I tried to help her see that what was important was how she responded to him. Would she quit or stay?

We went through the reasons for quitting. I told her I would not blame her if she decided to quit because she had been treated unfairly. It was only a game and there would be other softball seasons. She could even join another softball team or participate in other sports. Quitting made some sense, I assured her.

But I also stressed that she had worked the entire season for the team, had made many friends, and was only a few games away from being undefeated. How would she feel if she walked away from all that? She deserved to finish the season as part of the winning team she had helped create. "Don't let the coach or anyone else take that away from you, if that's what you really want" was my motherly

175

advice. I told her to think about it for a few days and assured her I would support her decision.

She decided to stay on the team and finish the season. Believe me, going to the next practice was not easy. I could see how apprehensive she was and I fully expected we would be shunned. Fortunately, I was wrong. The girls picked up right where they left off and probably had forgotten everything that happened three days earlier. Young children can be so "here and now" in their orientation to life. And to my amazement, a few other parents were solicitous of me and actually sat with me in the bleachers. The coach also was very friendly toward Mary and showed more interest in her than he had all season. None of us talked about that afternoon, but I was relieved the coach and other parents had welcomed her back.

Mary's trophy and team picture from the season sit on our living room shelf, a reminder of the small triumph of one little eight-year-old Black girl who is learning to cope with racial inequality. When the coach called at the start of the next season to ask her to join the team, however, Mary decided she did not want to play. Fair enough, I thought. I heard her tell the coach over the phone, "Thank you for asking, but I want to play soccer this year." In the end, she held fast to her dignity.

Mary learned an invaluable lesson from the footrace incident, but she also taught the coach, other parents, and me something, too. The coach and parents may be more sensitive to racial differences because of that afternoon. As for me, I am learning day after day what an incredible strength it takes for my daughter and all people of color to survive the challenge of racism.[143] Racism is like a cobweb, a sticky anathema to humanity.

In the earlier days of my journey across the color line, I often wished I could get away from the struggle, take a break, let my guard down, sleep peacefully. Racism continues to shape my daughter's and my life, just as it shapes the lives of all Black people and every White person who loves them or cares deeply about ending racism. Unlike those earlier days, however, I now accept that racism will outlive my daughter and me. We will do what we can in our lifetimes to help the racial equality movement, but we also will not let racism defeat us or take the joy out of life. Our love for each other is much too strong to allow our spirits to be broken. Someday, there will be enough of the "right people" to spiritually transform America and it will see the promise of racial equality achieved.

NOTES

1. One thought, somewhat humorous to those in legal education, came from Professor Patricia Williams's story in which she was accused of confusing everyone by using too much critical race theory in a trial. Patricia J. Williams, *The Alchemy of Race and Rights* (Cambridge, Mass.: Harvard University Press, 1991), 108.

2. Paul Brest, "Foreword: In Defense of the Antidiscrimination Principle," *Harvard Law Review* 90, no. 1 (1976): 7–8; Charles R. Lawrence, III, "The Id, the Ego and Equal Protection: Reckoning with Unconscious Racism," *Stanford Law Review* 39 (1987): 317.

3. Comment from an audience member at a conference sponsored by the Gainesville Commission on the Status of Women on "Violence against Women," April 30, 1998.

4. bell hooks, *Killing Rage: Ending Racism* (New York: Henry Holt & Co., 1995), 158.

5. See Stephanie M. Wildman and Adrienne D. Davis, "Making Systems of Privilege Visible," in *Privilege Revealed: How Invisible Preference Undermines America,* Stephanie M. Wildman, ed. (New York: New York University Press, 1996), 17 [hereinafter, *Privilege Revealed*](footnotes omitted).

6. Wildman and Davis, *Privilege Revealed,* 19–20.

7. There is actually a science of "space geography" (the study of the social construction of space) and scientists have conducted studies that reveal that involuntarily "segregated space [can] correlate to lack of power and knowledge on the part of the excluded group." Stephanie M. Wildman, "Privilege in the Workplace: The Missing Element in Antidiscrimination Law," in *Privilege Revealed,* supra note 5 at 27 (footnote omitted).

8. See Noel Ignatiev, "Treason to Whiteness Is Loyalty to Humanity," in *Critical White Studies: Looking behind the Mirror,* Richard Delgado and Jean Stefancic, eds. (Philadelphia: Temple University Press, 1997), 607–608. ("So-called whites have special responsibilities to abolition that only they can fulfill. Only

they can dissolve the white race from within, by rejecting the poisoned bait of white-skin privileges.")

9. Ignatiev, *Critical White Studies,* 610 (referring to the World War II slogan "An injury to one is an injury to all" as a motivator for repudiating white privilege). See also Anthony E. Cook, "Beyond Critical Legal Studies: The Reconstructive Theology of Dr. Martin Luther King, Jr.," *Harvard Law Review* 103 (1990): 985 (exploring the need to develop strategies for the common good of all people in the struggle for racial equality).

10. W. E. B. Du Bois, *The Souls of Black Folk* (New York: Signet Classic Penguin, 1969 [1903]), xxxi.

11. Du Bois, *The Souls of Black Folk,* xxxiii.

12. See Robert A. Williams, Jr., "Vampires Anonymous and Critical Race Practice," *Michigan Law Review* 95 (1997): 741, 756. ("[G]o out and make a difference in the world. Or, think independently, act for others. Whatever, you were taught your responsibilities, you know what it is you have to do.")

13. When Anthony Cook and I were on the same faculty, I used to attend his church and listen to his sermons about the role of law in developing goodwill toward others. My daughter was only one year old and Anthony, his family, and his congregation helped me begin my journey of love across the color line. He now teaches at a different university and his lessons come to me largely through his writings but with equal inspiration. See, e.g., Anthony E. Cook, *The Least of These* (New York: Routledge, 1996); "The Death of God in American Pragmatism and Realism: Resurrecting the Value of Love in Contemporary Jurisprudence," *Georgetown Law Journal* 82 (1994): 1431.

14. hooks, *Killing Rage* (1995), supra note 4 at 269.

15. hooks, *Killing Rage,* 270.

16. hooks, *Killing Rage,* 271.

17. For an excellent analysis of the dynamic of agency in sex discrimination, see Kathryn Abrams, "Sex Wars Redux: Agency and Coercion in Feminist Legal Theory," *Columbia Law Review* 95 (1995): 365; see also Katherine Franke, "What's Wrong with Sexual Harassment?" *Stanford Law Review* 49 (1997): 691 (exploring agency concept in same-sex harassment cases).

18. Wildman and Davis, *Privilege Revealed,* supra note 5 at 11.

19. hooks, *Killing Rage,* supra note 4 at 49.

20. See, e.g., Juan F. Perea, "The Black/White Paradigm of Race: The 'Normal Science' of American Racial Thought," *California Law Review* 85 (1997): 1219; *la Raza Law Journal* 10 (1997):133 (suggesting that focus on Black/White race issues marginalizes other racial groups). But see Anthony Paul Farley, "The Black Body as Fetish Object," *Oregon Law Review* 76 (1997): 457.

21. Professor Frank Valdes suggests the concept of "rotating centers" allows one to focus on one type of oppression at a time without diminishing the importance of focusing on other types of oppression and learning how different types of oppression work together. See Frank Valdes, Remarks, "Confronting Race," Conference, University of Florida Center for the Study of Race and Race Relations, February 20–21, 1998 (videotape on file with Media Center, University of Florida College of Law). Professors Trina Grillo and Stephanie Wildman use a similar concept of "recognition time," which they explain: "Recognition time acknowledges both the need to honor the pain of those oppressed by other isms, each in their turn, and the need to allow the oppression being focused on to remain center stage." Trina Grillo and Stephanie M. Wildman, "Obscuring the Importance of Race: The Implication of Making Comparisons between Racism and Sexism (or Other Isms)," in *Privilege Revealed,* supra note 5 at 99.

22. See, generally, Winthrop Jordan, *White Over Black: American Attitudes toward the Negro* (New York: W. W. Norton, 1968).

23. Dorothy Roberts, *Killing the Black Body: Race, Reproduction, and the Meaning of Liberty* (New York: Pantheon Books, 1997). See also D. Marvin Jones, "Darkness Made Visible: Law, Metaphor, and the Racial Self," *Georgetown Law Journal* 82 (1993): 437, 471–478 (role of color in defining race).

24. Perea, "The Black/White Paradigm of Race," supra note 20 at 1237, 1256.

25. This story appeared in my article "If Black Is So Special, Then Why Isn't It in the Rainbow?" *Connecticut Law Review* 26 (1994): 1195.

26. See Frances E. Kendall, *Diversity in the Classroom: A Multicultural Approach to the Education of Young Children* (New York: Teachers College Press, 1983), 20 (research supports findings that children express positive and negative feelings about racial differences by age three or four).

27. Christine B. Hickman, "The Devil and the One Drop Rule: Racial Categories, African Americans, and the U.S. Census," *Michigan Law Review* 95 (1997): 1161.

28. Joe R. Feagin and Hernan Vera, *White Racism* (New York and London: Routledge Press, 1995), 137.

29. Randall Robinson, *Defending the Spirit: A Black Life in America* (New York: Dutton, 1998), 54–55.

30. Theresa Glennon, "Race, Education, and the Construction of a Disabled Class," *Wisconsin Law Review* (1995): 1237.

31. I tell this story in my article "The Heart of Equal Protection: Education and Race," *N.Y.U. Review of Law & Social Change* 23, no. 1 (1997): 50–51.

32. Joe R. Feagin and Melvin P. Sikes, *Living with Racism: The Black Middle-Class Experience* (Boston: Beacon Press, 1994), 37–77.

33. W. E. B. Du Bois, *The Souls of Black Folk* (New York: Signet Classic Penguin, 1969 [1903]), xxxix.

34. This story is developed in "The Make-Believe World of Colorblindness: Not What Our Children Need," in *Gender and Race on Campus and in the School: Beyond Affirmative Action* (Washington, D.C.: American Association of University Women, 1997).

35. "The Make-Believe World of Colorblindness," 339.

36. hooks, *Killing Rage,* supra note 4 at 185.

37. See, e.g., Derrick Bell, *And We Are Not Saved* (New York: Basic Books, Inc., 1987); hooks, *Killing Rage,* supra note 4; Feagin and Sikes, *Living with Racism,* supra note 32; Stephen Steinberg, *Turning Back: The Retreat from Racial Justice in American Thought and Policy* (Boston: Beacon Press, 1995); David K. Shipler, *A Country of Strangers: Blacks and Whites in America* (New York: Knopf, 1997).

38. Martin Luther King, Jr., "Letter from a Birmingham Jail," in *I Have a Dream: Writings and Speeches That Changed the World,* James Melvin Washington, ed. (San Francisco: Harper, 1992), 91. See also Steinberg, *Turning Back,* supra note 37 at 134.

39. "U-Fla. Leader Keeps Job after Apology For Racial Remark," *Washington Post,* January 28, 1998, A6 ("Around the Nation"); John Lombardi, "To: Students, Faculty, Staff, Alumni and Friends," *Independent Florida Alligator,* January 20, 1998, 1.

40. Feagin and Sikes, *Living with Racism,* supra note 32 at 3.

41. hooks, *Killing Rage,* supra note 4 at 114–115 (critiquing representation of Black characters in media: "[Black] subordination is made to appear 'natural' because most black characters are consistently portrayed as always a little less ethical and moral than whites, not given to rational reasonable action"). See also Cheryl I. Harris, "Whiteness as Property," *Harvard Law Review* 106 (1993): 1709, 1757. See, generally, A. Leon Higginbotham, *Shades of Freedom: Racial Politics and Presumptions of the American Legal Process* (New York: Oxford University Press, 1996).

42. Most White Americans think that discrimination is no longer significant in America. Feagin and Sikes, *Living with Racism,* supra note 32 at 11. However, studies show that a majority of Whites consider race in making important decisions such as: "choosing neighborhoods, employees, business partners, places to go in the city, and mates for themselves and their children." Feagin and Sikes, *Living with* Racism, 23.

43. See Christine Leon, "UF Launches Race Relations Center with Symposium," *Independent Florida Alligator,* February 23, 1998, 1. The Honorable Susan H. Black, Circuit Judge, United States Court of Appeals for the Eleventh Cir-

cuit, who earned her J.D. from the University of Florida College of Law in 1967, has commented publicly (and with a smile) about the customary jingling of keys and shuffling of feet by male classmates when women spoke in law school classrooms. Judge Black's comments were made at a reception honoring the University of Florida's Women of Distinction at the College of Law in the Fall, 1997.

44. Kevin Eckhardt, "Opinions: Key-Jingling Meant to Silence Irrelevance," *Independent Florida Alligator,* February 24, 1998, 7.

45. Paul Mascia, "Opinions: Perception Is Our Problem," *Independent Florida Alligator,* February 27, 1998, 7.

46. See Exec. Order No. 11,246, 3 C.F.R. § 301 (1964–65) as amended by Exec. Order No. 12,086, 41 C.F.R. §§ 602.10, et seq. (1986).

47. Steinberg, *Turning Back,* supra note 37 at 166–167. ("[A]ffirmative action was never a desideratum pursued for its own sake, but rather a policy of last resort. . . .")

48. Steinberg, *Turning Back,* 167–68.

49. Steinberg, *Turning Back,* 114 (quoting President Johnson's "To Fulfill These Rights," addressed to the Howard University graduating class on June 4, 1965). Professor Steinberg compares Johnson's speech, written by Richard Goodwin and Daniel Patrick Moynihan, with the following passage from a 1956 book:

Overt job discrimination is only one of the important hurdles which must be overcome before color can disappear as a determining factor in the lives and fortunes of men. . . . The prevailing view among social scientists holds that there are no significant differences among groups as to the distribution of innate aptitudes or at most very slight differences. On the other hand, differences among individuals are very substantial. The extent to which an individual is able to develop his aptitudes will largely depend upon the circumstances present in the family within which he grows up and the opportunities which he encounters at school and in the larger community. (Eli Ginzberg, *The Negro Potential* [New York: Columbia University Press, 1956], 7.)

50. Steinberg, *Turning Back,* supra note 37 at 115.

51. Feagin and Sikes, *Living with Racism,* supra note 32 at 319.

52. U.S. Const. amend. XIV.

53. Civil Rights Act of 1964, 42 U.S.C. §§ 2000a et seq. (1964).

54. 42 U.S.C. § 1983.

55. john a. powell, "An Agenda for the Post–Civil Rights Era," *University*

of San Francisco Law Review 29 (1995): 889, 903 (discounting the color-blind doctrine that suggests that because the government's explicitly sponsored racism is largely a thing of the past, so must racism be a thing of the past).

56. Perhaps it may be obvious (certainly, it is obvious at least from the perspective of a person of color) that in a nonracist society, absence of persons of color in these positions would not have lasted for so long. But see Daniel A. Farber and Suzanna Sherry, *Beyond All Reason: The Radical Assault on Truth in American Law* (New York: Oxford University Press, 1997).

57. Steinberg, *Turning Back,* supra note 37 at 116.

58. Steinberg, *Turning Back.* Semantic infiltration is one part of the general "backlash" phenomenon common in most struggles for equality. The "backlash" occurs when the dominant group demands that "center stage" be restored to them because the subordinated groups are receiving too much attention and accommodation in their struggle. In the context of race, Professors Grillo and Wildman state, "White supremacy creates in whites the expectation that issues of concern to them will be central in every discourse." Trina Grillo and Stephanie M. Wildman, "Obscuring the Importance of Race: The Implication of Making Comparisons between Racism and Sexism (or Other Isms)," in *Privilege Revealed,* supra note 5 at 91. For an analysis of the same concept in the context of sex equality, see Susan Faludi, *Backlash: The Undeclared War against Women* (New York: Crown Pub., Inc., 1991).

59. See *Regents of the University of California v. Bakke,* 438 U.S. 265, 413 (1978) (Stevens, J., dissenting).

60. Secretly, many goodwill Whites might see the selection of a minority as a step backward away from merit.

61. See Robert L. Hayman and Nancy Levit, "The Constitutional Ghetto," *Wisconsin Law Review* (1993): 627, 678–679. The economic disparities reflect something beyond a recurring and exceptional set of coincidences. See "The United States," *American Economic Review* 77 (1987): 316, 319 (surveying empirical studies and finding that "even when fairly refined measures of productivity-related characteristics are held constant, blacks and women earn less than whites and men").

62. Robert L. Hayman and Nancy Levit, "The Constitutional Ghetto."

63. Joe R. Feagin, *Racist America: Roots, Current Realities, and Future Reparations* (New York: Routledge Press, 2000).

64. *Brown v. Board of Education,* 347 U.S. 483 (1954).

65. See Sharon Elizabeth Rush, "The Heart of Equal Protection: Education and Race," *N.Y.U. Review of Law & Social Change* 23, no. 1 (1997): 2–7.

66. See Gary Orfield, Mark D. Bachmeier, David R. James, and Tamela

Eitle, *Deepening Segregation in American Public Schools* (Cambridge, Mass.: Harvard Project on School Desegregation, 1997).

67. See, generally, Jonathan Kozol, *Savage Inequalities: Children in America's Schools* (New York: HarperCollins, 1991), (examining the disparities between wealthy and poor public school districts). The Supreme Court held in *Missouri v. Jenkins,* 495 U.S. 33 (1995), that a school district did not have to continue to fund quality public education programs in an attempt to improve standardized test scores of students in a predominantly Black school. For an analysis of *Missouri v. Jenkins,* see Bradley W. Joondeph, *"Missouri v. Jenkins* and the De Facto Abandonment of Court-Enforced Desegregation," *Washington Law Review* 71 (1996): 597. See, generally, Robin D. Barnes, "Black America and School Choice: Charting a New Course," *Yale Law Journal* 106 (1997): 2375, 2381 (exploring how charter schools "offer a viable option for the effective education of black children" in light of integration's failure).

68. Andrew Hacker, *Two Nations: Black and White, Separate, Hostile, Unequal* (New York: Ballantine Books, 1995).

69. hooks, *Killing Rage,* supra note 4 passim. See, generally, Kenneth B. Nunn, "Law as a Eurocentric Enterprise," *Journal of Law & Inequality* 25 (1997): 323.

70. Steinberg, *Turning Back,* supra note 37 at 75 (quoting Stokely Carmichael and Charles V. Hamilton, *Black Power: The Politics of Liberation in America* [New York: Random House, 1967], 4).

71. Steinberg, *Turning Back,* supra note 37 at 76 (quoting Stokely Carmichael and Charles V. Hamilton, *Black Power: The Politics of Liberation in America,* 4).

72. A. Leon Higginbotham, *Shades of Freedom: Racial Politics and Presumptions of the American Legal Process* (New York: Oxford University Press, 1996).

73. Steinberg, *Turning Back,* supra note 37 at 29 (citing Samuel George Morton, *Crania Americana*).

74. Richard J. Herrnstein and Charles Murray, *The Bell Curve: Intelligence and Class Structure in American Life* (New York: Free Press, 1995).

75. Affirmative action policies have been extended to other racial minorities and also women, consistent with Title VII's general prohibition against racial, ethnic, and sex discrimination and also consistent with society's growing commitment to equality for people of color and women.

76. Paul Finkelman, "The Rise of the New Racism," *Yale Law & Policy Review* 15 (1996): 245, 281 (critiquing Dinesh D'Souza's book *The End of Racism: Principles for a Multiracial Society* [New York: Free Press, 1995] as a "big lie." Id. at 246).

77. *Dred Scott v. Sanford,* 60 U.S. (19 How.) 393 (1857).

78. Lynne N. Henderson, "Legality and Empathy," *Michigan Law Review* 85 (1987): 1574; Cynthia V. Ward, "A Kinder, Gentler Liberalism: Visions of Empathy in Feminist and Communitarian Literature," *University of Chicago Law Review* 61 (1995): 930.

79. I do not think repudiating privilege is motivated by altruism, which implies that only kindness is behind the act. This would make Blacks' equality with Whites dependent on Whites' kindness. Rather, repudiation is built on the idea of rejecting the underlying premise of a transaction. A person of goodwill would be inclined to repudiate White privilege because she is a person of goodwill toward others and she understands her privilege was wrongfully obtained through the heinous subordination of Blacks. Her repudiation is not a gift to Blacks; her repudiation is an act of harmonizing her self-identity with her sincere goodwill toward others.

80. Derrick Bell, Jr., "Racism Is Here to Stay: Now What?" *Howard Law Journal* 35 (1991): 790.

81. Dinesh D'Souza, *The End of Racism: Principles for a Multiracial Society* (New York: Free Press, 1995), 2, 67–114. An excellent critique by Paul Finkelman, "The Rise of the New Racism," *Yale Law & Policy Review* 15 (1996): 245, summarizes a 700-page journey through the arguments supporting White denial.

82. Stephan Thernstrom and Abigail Thernstrom, *America in Black and White: One Nation, Indivisible* (New York: Simon & Schuster, 1997).

83. Arlene F. Saluter, "Marital Status and Living Arrangements: March 1992," in U.S. Dept. of Commerce, Current Population Reports, Population Characteristics X (December 1992) (the number of interracial marriages was reported as 1,161,000).

84. Jane Gross, "UC Berkeley at Crux of New Multiracial Consciousness," *L.A. Times,* January 9, 1996, A1.

85. Linda Mathews, "More Than Identity Rides on New Racial Category," *N.Y. Times,* July 6, 1996, A1.

86. Alexis de Tocqueville, *Democracy in America,* vol. 1 (New York: Vintage Books, 1990), 374.

87. Professor Cheryl I. Harris has written the best exposition of this phenomenon and its relationship to property laws in "Whiteness as Property," *Harvard Law Review* 106 (1993): 1709.

88. Professor Christine B. Hickman persuasively argues that the "drop of Black blood" rule has become a source of Black power in her pathbreaking article "The Devil and the One Drop Rule: Racial Categories, African Americans, and the U.S. Census," *Michigan Law Review* 95 (1997): 1161, 1166. ("The Devil

fashioned [the one drop rule] out of racism, malice, greed, lust, and ignorance, but in so doing he also accomplished good: His rule created the African-American race as we know it today.")

89. For a critique of the myth of Black men raping White women as the primary rape statistic, see Jennifer Wriggins, "Rape, Racism and the Law," *Harvard Women's Law Journal* 6 (1983): 103.

90. Lynching also was a common response. See Barbara Holden-Smith, "Lynching, Federalism, and the Intersection of Race and Gender in the Progressive Era," *Yale Law Journal and Feminism* 8 (1996): 31.

91. See Edward Lazarus, *Closed Chambers: The First Eyewitness Account of the Epic Struggles Inside the Supreme Court* (New York: Times Book, 1998), 77–81. See, generally, Dan T. Carter, *Scottsboro: A Tragedy Of the American South,* rev. ed. (Baton Rouge: Louisiana State University Press, 1979); James Goodman, *Stories of Scottsboro* (New York: Pantheon, 1994).

92. Lazarus, *Closed Chambers,* supra note 91 at 81.

93. Lazarus, *Closed Chambers,* 91. He also notes that Blacks made up only 12 percent of the population.

94. Irene Sege, "Race, Violence Make Complex Picture," *Boston Globe,* January 31, 1990, National/Foreign Sec., 1.

95. Kimberle Crenshaw, "Demarginalizing the Intersection of Race and Sex: A Black Feminist Critique of Antidiscrimination Doctrine, Feminist Theory and Antiracist Politics," *University of Chicago Legal Forum* (1989): 139.

96. Cheryl I. Harris, "Finding Sojourner's Truth: Race, Gender and the Institution of Property," *Cardozo Law Review* 18 (1996): 309, 313.

97. *Loving v. Virginia,* 388 U.S. 1 (1967).

98. Hickman, "The Devil and the One Drop Rule," supra note 88 at 1164, n. 10. ("[A] 1994 poll showed that 14.7% of White Americans still favor a law making interracial marriage illegal," citing "Up from Separatism," *Economist,* October 21, 1995, 30.) See, generally, Randall Kennedy, "How Are We Doing with Loving?: Race, Law, and Intermarriage," *Boston University Law Review* 77 (1997): 815 (exploring impediments to Black/White marriages, although supportive of them).

99. See Shipler, *A Country of Strangers,* supra note 37 at 115–116. ("Not all objection to interracial dating comes from whites. In the spirit of black pride, black solidarity, black cultural cohesion, some blacks also resist and resent.")

100. In an analogous context, heterosexual love has not dismantled patriarchy. In fact, many feminist scholars posit that heterosexual "love" maintains patriarchy. As Professor Catharine MacKinnon admonishes, "Heterosexuality is [patriarchy's] social structure, desire its internal dynamic, gender and family its

congealed forms, sex roles its qualities generalized to social personal, reproduction a consequence, and control its issue." Catherine A. MacKinnon, *Toward a Feminist Theory of the State* (Cambridge and London: Harvard University Press, 1989), 3–4. Professor bell hooks writes that "[p]atriarchy is about domination." hooks, *Killing Rage,* supra note 4 at 73.

101. Joan C. Williams, "Deconstructing Gender," *Michigan Law Review* 87 (1989): 797, 843.

102. The National Association of Black Social Workers took the position in 1972 that "Black children should be placed only with Black families" primarily in its belief that this policy was in the child's best interest and that it also protected Black cultural identity. See Rita James Simon and Howard Altstein, *Transracial Adoption* (New York; Westport, Conn. and London: Praeger, 1987), 9 (quoting from the National Association of Black Soc. Workers, Position Paper [1972]).

103. The arguments against adoption of Black children by White parents are explored in Jacqueline Macaulay and Stewart Macaulay, "Adoption for Black Children: A Case Study of Expert Discretion," *Review of Law & Society* 1 (1978): 265, 280–305. But see Elizabeth Bartholet, "Where Do Black Children Belong? The Politics of Race Matching in Adoption," *University of Pennsylvania Law Review* 139 (1991): 1163.

104. The assimilation problem has been articulated most poignantly in the context of school integration and the failure of *Brown.* See, e.g., Jerome McCristal Culp, Jr., "Black People in White Face: Assimilation, Culture, and the Brown Case," *William & Mary Law Review* 36 (1995): 665.

105. R. Richard Banks, "The Color of Desire: Fulfilling Adoptive Parents' Racial Preferences through Discriminatory State Action," *Yale Law Journal* 107 (1998): 875.

106. Bartholet, "Where Do Black Children Belong?" supra note 103 at 1223–1226 (delay in placement can cause psychological trauma).

107. Elizabeth Bartholet, *Family Bonds: Adoption and the Politics of Parenting* (Boston and New York: Houghton Mifflin, 1993), 96.

108. Bartholet, "Where Do Black Children Belong?" supra note 103 at 1211–1216, 1221–1225.

109. Twila L. Perry, "The Transracial Adoption Controversy: An Analysis of Discourse and Subordination," *N.Y.U. Review Law & Social Change* 21 (1993): 33, 57–59 (criticizing studies suggesting Black children suffer no harm from being raised by White parents).

110. The Small Business Jobs Protection Act, Pub. L. No. 104–188, S 1808(a)(3)(1966), reads:

[N]either the State nor any other entity in the State that receives funds from the Federal Government and is involved in adoption or foster care placements may—(A) deny to any person the opportunity to become an adoptive or a foster parent, on the basis of race, color, or national origin of the person, or of the child, involved; or (B) delay or deny the placement of a child for adoption or into foster care, on the basis of the race, color, or national origin of the adoptive or foster parent, or the child, involved.

111. hooks, *Killing Rage,* supra note 4 at 27.

112. hooks, *Killing Rage.*

113. See, e.g., Judd F. Sneirson, "Black Rage and the Criminal Law: A Principled Approach to a Polarized Debate," *University of Pennsylvania Law Review* 143(1995): 2251, 2260–2262 (brief overview of justification and excuse defenses in criminal law); see, generally, Paul Harris, *Black Rage Confronts the Law* (New York: New York University Press, 1997), 2–7; Patricia J. Falk, "Novel Theories of Criminal Defense Based upon the Toxicity of the Social Environment: Urban Psychosis, Television Intoxication, and Black Rage," *North Carolina Law Review* 74 (1996): 731, 748–757.

114. William H. Grier and Price M. Cobbs, *Black Rage* (New York: Basic Books, 1968).

115. Sneirson, "Black Rage and the Criminal Law," supra note 113.

116. Sneirson, "Black Rage and the Criminal Law," 2252.

117. The contrary view is presented by Professor Alan Dershowitz who posits that "the 'black rage' variation on the abuse-excuse defense is an insult to millions of law-abiding black Americans." Alan M. Dershowitz, *The Abuse Excuse and Other Cop-Outs, Sob Stories and Evasions Of Responsibility* (Boston: Little, Brown, 1994), 90.

118. See, e.g., Florida Statute, Ch. 827.03 (1997).

119. Tocqueville, *Democracy in America,* vol. 1, supra note 86 at 380.

120. Donald R. Kinder and Lynn M. Sanders, *Divided by Color: Racial Politics and Democratic Ideals* (Chicago and London: University of Chicago Press, 1996), 103 (footnote omitted).

121. Kinder and Sanders, *Divided by Color.*

122. Deborah W. Post, "Race, Riots and the Rule of Law," *Denver University Law Review* 70 (1993): 237, 255. For an excellent critique of the meaning of the riots, see Juan F. Perea, "Los Olvidados: On the Making of Invisible People," *N.Y.U. Law Review* 70 (1995): 965.

123. Joe R. Feagin and Hernan Vera, *White Racism,* supra note 28 at 83–84, 97.

124. Kinder and Sanders, *Divided by Color,* supra note 120 at 104. See, generally, Thernstrom and Thernstrom, supra note 82 at 39.

125. Paul Butler, "Racially Based Jury Nullification: Black Power in the Criminal Justice System," *Yale Law Journal* 105 (1995): 677, 679; see also Darryl K. Brown, "Jury Nullification within the Rule of Law," *Minnesota Law Review* 81 (1997): 1149.

126. Paul Butler, "(Color) Blind Faith: The Tragedy of Race, Crime, and the Law," *Harvard Law Review* 111 (1998): 1270, 1285–1286. See also Sheri Lynn Johnson, "Respectability, Race Neutrality, and Truth," *Yale Law Journal* 107 (1998): 2619; Kenneth B. Nunn, "Rights Held Hostage: Race Ideology and the Peremptory Challenge," *Harvard Civil Rights—Civil Liberties Law Review* 28 (1993): 63 (both analyzing racial injustice throughout the criminal justice system).

127. See, e.g., Andrew D. Leipold, "The Dangers of Race-Based Jury Nullification: A Response to Prof. Butler," *UCLA Law Review* 44 (1996): 109; Richard St. John, "License to Nullify: The Democratic and Constitutional Deficiencies of Authorized Jury Lawmaking," *Yale Law Journal* 106 (1997): 2563.

128. See Randall Kennedy, *Race, Crime and the Law* (New York: Pantheon Books, 1997).

129. Butler, "(Color) Blind Faith," supra note 126 at 1282 (quoting from Kennedy, supra note 128 at 20).

130. Butler, "(Color) Blind Faith," supra note 126 at 1283.

131. Kinder and Sanders, supra note 120 at 103. ("If the civil rights movement and the flagrantly racist reaction it incited compelled many white Americans to express their support for racial equality as a matter of principle, the riots and the new belligerent rhetoric pushed them in quite a different direction . . . In the view of many white Americans, the problem of race was solved.")

132. See Perea, *Black-White Paradigm of Race,* supra note 122 at 967 (footnote omitted). See Anthony V. Alfieri, "Defending Racial Violence," *Columbia Law Review* 95 (1995): 1301 (analysis of the rhetoric of race in trials involving racial violence).

133. Shipler, *A Country of Strangers,* supra note 37 at 397.

134. Shipler, *A Country of Strangers,* 400.

135. Shipler, *A Country of Strangers.* ("After the jury made its decision, a *Washington Post* poll found that 85 percent of blacks and 34 percent of whites agreed with the verdict; 8 percent of blacks and 55 percent of whites disagreed.")

136. Although the acquittal of O. J. Simpson in his trial for allegedly murdering Nicole Brown Simpson and Ronald Goldman did not inspire Whites to riot, his acquittal did enrage most White Americans, who felt he got away with murder. That was disturbing enough to many White Americans, but their anger was exacerbated in the O.J. case because most Whites believed Simpson's lawyer,

Johnnie Cochran, deliberately and inappropriately played "the race card." Specifically, some Whites believed that Cochran obscured the question of O.J.'s guilt or innocence by turning the case into a conspiracy by the White police officers and detectives against O.J. For most White Americans, the idea that the White officers would be involved in a conspiracy against Blacks was preposterous and deeply offensive.

Compounding their sense of outrage at the allegations of a conspiracy within the specific context of the Simpson trial was a more generalized feeling by many White Americans that Black America attributed the White officers' alleged racist motivations to any White who believed O.J. committed the murders. Somehow, the allegations of the officer's conspiracy against O.J. translated into an accusation that White America, particularly its criminal justice system, was "out to get" Black Americans, especially Black men. The ugliness and absurdity of the allegation that White America is racist made many Whites defensive and angry. Any possible relationship between White police officer conduct in the O.J. investigation and White police officer conduct in Los Angeles and elsewhere toward Blacks, Latinos, and people of other colors never got explored in the broader context of institutional racism. Rather, the allegations of White police officer racism could simply be dismissed as irrational in the context of O.J.'s case because it was so obvious to White society that he was guilty. See, generally, Devon Carbado, "The Construction of O. J. Simpson as a Racial Victim," *Harvard Civil Rights—Civil Liberties Law Review* 32 (1997): 49; George Fischer, "The O.J. Simpson Corpus," *Stanford Law Review* 49 (1997): 971.

137. Proposition 209 states: "The state shall not discriminate against or grant preferential treatment to any individual or group on the basis of race, sex, color, ethnicity, or national origin in the operation of public employment, public education, or public contracting." California Constitution, Art. 1, Section 31 (a). Ward Connerly, a University of California regent and a Black man, is the leader behind the Proposition 209 movement. See Louis Freedberg, "UC Law Schools at Wit's End as Minorities Go Elsewhere," *San Francisco Chronicle,* July 18, 1997, A1. Because Proposition 209 is supported by a Black person, some people will be inclined to summarily dismiss any possibility that Proposition 209 passed because the recent racial unrest was making Whites too uncomfortable. Blacks often disagree on many issues and Ward Connerly is entitled to oppose affirmative action, just as Whites are given that option. See Angela Harris, "Race and Essentialism in Feminist Legal Theory," *Stanford Law Review* 42 (1990): 581. Simultaneously, the fact of his Blackness is relevant precisely because many Whites think in essentialist terms. See Leslie Espinoza, "Masks and Other Disguises: Exposing Legal Academia," *Harvard Law Review* 103 (1990): 1878 (taking excep-

tion to Professor Randall Kennedy's position that being Black does not give one a "special vantage point," in his article, "Racial Critiques of Legal Academia," *Harvard Law Review* 102 (1989): 1745.) The point, of course, is that Proposition 209 passed because a lot of White voters supported it and they may have been influenced by the fact of Ward Connerly's race.

138. See Carl Rowan, "Scholastic Genocide," *Denver Post,* May 24, 1997, B7 (enrollment of Black and Hispanic students in law and medical schools in Texas and California reported to be down 81 percent and 50 percent, respectively).

139. See Thomas S. Mulligan, "Texaco Bias Case Decision Has Glass Ceilings Rattling Workplace: Employees Claiming Discrimination Get More Attention," *L.A. Times,* December 8, 1996, D1.

140. *Brown v. Board of Education of Topeka,* 347 U.S. 483, 494 (1954).

141. Feagin and Sikes, *Living with Racism,* supra note 28.

142. I began to develop the ideas presented here in an essay, "Doing Antiracism: Making an Egalitarian Future," coauthored with Joe Feagin and Jacqueline Johnson, forthcoming in *Contemporary Sociology* (2000).

143. Peggy C. Davis, "Law as Microaggression," *Yale Law Journal* 98 (1989): 1559 (exploring day-to-day effects of racism—ironically, this came out the year my daughter was born).

ABOUT THE AUTHOR

SHARON E. RUSH received her B.A. and J.D. from Cornell University. She is currently the Irving Cypen Professor of Law at Fredric G. Levin College of Law at the University of Florida, where she also is cofounder of the Center for the Study of Race and Race Relations. She specializes in constitutional law and has written numerous articles on race and race relations.